# The
# DISCIPLESHIP
# SERIES

**A COMPREHENSIVE OUTLINE OF BIBLE STUDY NOTES**

## Taka Sande

Unless otherwise indicated, all scripture quotations are from the *King James Version* of the Bible.

The Discipleship Series
© Copyright 2012 by Taka Sande

ISBN 978 0 620 53564 9

For permission requests, please contact the author directly at:
**Taka Sande**
Telephone   +27 72 324 2008
E-mail        admin@itsmyfootprint.com
Website      http://www.itsmyfootprint.com/

This book is designed to provide information about the subject-matter covered. Every effort has been made to make this book as complete and accurate as possible. However, there may be mistakes both typographical and in content. Therefore, the text should be used only as a general guide and not as the ultimate source of the subject matter covered.

Cover Design by: **Vimbai Jacha**
Edited by: **Trudie Winter**

# DEDICATION

*To all the pilgrims who need the help of the good shepherd.*

# FOREWORD

"The Discipleship Series is a wonderful teaching aid for every church leader. Ideal for home group Bible study, church Bible study and general fellowship discussion with family and friends.

The series is a complete message of the Bible simplified for easy understanding and at the same time immensely enriching. Each Bible topic is well explained to cater for both the young and the mature Christians.

Taka has made it very simple and exiting to study and teach the word of God in this series. When I began to read I found myself in deep devotion, and study at the same time.

The topics covered are all complete for those intending to grow in the knowledge of the word of God seriously. This is a fantastic tool for daily devotion."

By: **Dr Rodwell Jacha**, Author, Minister, and Speaker

"It is the goal of every God-fearing individual to become like Christ, in thought, speech and deed. In order to effectively walk towards what God has ordained for your life, you need someone to hold you by your hand and guide your every step. This book shapes and guides you towards becoming the disciplined follower of Christ (a disciple).

It is always important to go back to the basics of faith and begin laying a firm foundation on which to build your life on. This exceptionally written masterpiece helps you to become a grounded, sound and effective Christian. You will become bold in proclaiming your faith. This is a book that every Christian needs".

By: **Rabison Shumba**, Consultant, Author, and Coach

# TABLE OF CONTENTS

## CONTENTS

# INTRODUCTION

Going back to the basics! No matter where we are or how long we have been there, the basic things must not be forgotten. Basic principles are the ones that make our foundations. And once in a while we go back to check our foundation, because the whole building sits on it. In this book I compiled basic Christian teachings that I have learned though sermons, courses and during self-study.

Before the Lord Jesus left He said in Matthew 28:19-20 NIV, *"Therefore go and make disciples of all nations, baptizing them in the name of the father and the Son and of the Holy Spirit, and teaching them to obey everything I have commanded you."* A disciple is a learner or a pupil. Jesus' desire is for us to make as many disciples as we can, who are taught and grounded in the word and knowledge of God, so that we have Christians who are like Jesus, in personal life speech and conduct.

There is a need for discipleship. There is a need for people to grow in the knowledge of the Lord, so that they can enjoy a victorious Christian life. This is why the Lord Jesus repeated three times to Peter, *"Do you love me [with a deep, instinctive, personal affection for me, as for a close friend]? ............ Feed My sheep"* John 21:15-19 Amp. Read John 21:15-19.

This series of teachings are a guideline for teachers or leaders of home groups, or Bible study groups, who want to serve and touch the heart of Jesus by 'feeding His sheep'. Furthermore, they are also useful for personal Bible study, and to grow in the knowledge of God. If you are a leader, the souls you lead are in your hands, do not let the blood be upon you. How can they do it when they have not heard! *"Do you truly love me? Feed my sheep."*

# 1. PERSONAL DEVOTIONAL LIFE

What is devotion? Why should we indulge in it? Time is precious. Time is money. Should we let it go just like that? Is talking to God the best way to spend it? Today it seems people have not enough time at their disposal. They need to go to work, go to school, watch TV, do sport, socialize, check something on the internet, eat, pray, sleep, read, etc. All this has to be done in 24 hours. We have a situation of too many events, chasing too little time. Prayer is one of the things that may not find a place on our list, yet it is the most important thing in our lives. So what should we do? Prioritize! Let us take a close look at it.

Devote means to set apart, to dedicate, or to consecrate. This word comes from devout, which means seriously religious, prayerfully, sincere or showing reverence. Some people call it a quiet, or secret time with God. It is a heart to heart talk between the Father and a son. It means setting yourself aside to sit at the feet of Jesus as we fellowship with Him. This involves praying to God as we talk to Him and read the Bible, the Word of God as He talks to us. It is not just being religious, but an exciting communion with God, sharing every intimate detail of our lives. It is also a time to listen to God attentively.

Personal devotion helps us in our day to day struggle with Satan. In Eph 6:12 the Bible reminds us that we are constantly in spiritual warfare. Spending time with the Lord refocuses and re-orientates, our minds so that we become alert and sensitive to the baits of Satan. How then do we go about this?

## Time and place
Choose an isolated place where there is minimum distraction. Remember this is a personal appointment with God. Often it is not the surroundings, but our own mind that can be our source of disturbance. Focus on Jesus and meditate on His word, not on your own thoughts. Set aside time regularly, for instant in the morning, but make it a habit. Let it become a way of life! Do not choose the times of the day when you are tired, and have nothing to do. Give God the best of your time. We do not have quiet time because we have nothing to do, but it is essential for our growth spiritually, as well as our wholeness.

Today all men who are being used mightily by God have a secret time with God. Even in the Bible great man of God had personal devotional times for example: Abraham [Gen 18:22; 19:27], David [Ps 5:3; 57:8; 108:2], Solomon [Prov 8:17], Isaiah [Isa 26:9] and even Jesus [Luke 4:42; 5:16; 6:12].

All these men, met the Lord early in the morning before sunrise. There are many people today who developed this habit, and are living victorious lives. Remember to go to bed early, if you want to meet the Lord early in the morning. Ask God to wake you up at the time you want to meet with Him.

## Bible Study During Personal Devotion

First you need study materials. The most essential items are:1) A Bible; for studying and meditation, 2) A journal and pen; to record what the Lord is teaching you and to write prayer requests. Memorize several verses as you read, and ponder on their implications for your life. It is advisable to have a system of studying your Bible e.g. by book, topic, using a program or character in the Bible. You may use a commentary on these notes. Progress, as you work slowly and thoughtfully through the Bible. Allow the Holy Spirit to speak to you. Obey Him when he shows you something. Finishing the whole Bible is not the aim, but for you to be transformed by meeting with God. These are some of the questions to ask yourself each time you finish:

1. What new things have I learned today?
2. Is there an example to follow?
3. Is there a new commandment for me to obey?
4. Is there any error for me to avoid?
5. Is there a sin for me to forsake, or a promise to claim?
6. Is there a new thought about God?

## Prayer in Personal Devotion

Pray out loud if it is possible. Even if you cannot, God does hear silent prayers. Your prayer should have these four elements ACTS that is:

Adoration: - Praise and worship the Lord – Ps 95:6.

Confession: - Repent. Forsake and confess every sin revealed – Ps 32:5.

Thanksgiving: - Give thanks to God for all his provision and works – Phil 4:6.

Supplication: - Intercession, petitions, requests and desires – 1Tim 2:1.

At first it will be difficult to concentrate on the Bible or pray, but do not give up. The devil does not want you to communicate with God, so he tries to frustrate you with all sorts of problems. Your interaction with God is your strength. It is surprisingly true, unlike us Christians, that the devil knows how powerful personal devotion is. That's why he makes you have reasons of not having some time with God. If you develop this practice over a period of time you will grow to enjoy it, as you discover the hidden things in the word of God, and how real our God is.

You will start to hear when God speaks to you and guide you throughout the day. As a result, you will start to live a fruitful life. Soon people will be asking you 'Why are you always happy and positive?'

# 2. PERSONAL VICTORY AND CHALLENGES

In order for a new Christian to maintain his/her testimony, there is a need for breakthrough. He needs to leave the past life [2 Cor 5:17], and overcome the forces of darkness attacking him [Eph 6:12]. To enjoy Christian life, he has to live victoriously in this newness of life, and this is often difficult for the new believer. In this section we will look at the snares used by the devil, and how to overcome them.

## Personality of man
The Bible classifies people into three categories:

I.   **The Natural man,** [1Cor 2:14], is an unregenerate man, a typical man, or an unsaved man. He does not possess the Holy Spirit, therefore he cannot evaluate [discern, judge] the things of the Spirit and see their truth, beauty, and excellence. He cannot know [understand] them. Therefore they are foolishness [absurd, silly, senseless, tasteless] to him, so he will not receive them but rejects them.

II.  **The Spirit man,** [1 Cor 2:14-16], is a born again consecrated Christian. He has the Holy Spirit, and is able to evaluate and understand "all things," both the things of man, and the things of the Spirit. Because he possesses both the human spirit and the Holy Spirit, he can evaluate and understand a natural man. Since a natural man does not possess the Holy Spirit, he cannot evaluate and understand a spiritual man.

III. **The Carnal man,** [1Cor3:1], is usually led by the flesh and not by the Spirit. He can only understand the things of the Spirit, unless they are presented to him in a simple [elementary] way. There are two kinds of carnal Christians: (1) New Carnal Christians [1 Cor 3:1], who are carnal [fleshly] because they are babies in Christ, having had no opportunity to grow in Christ. (2) Old Carnal Christians [1 Cor 3:3], who are carnal because they are still babies in Christ, even after having had full opportunity to grow in Christ. New carnal Christians cannot be blamed for their carnality. Old carnal Christians can be blamed for their carnality.

When Paul established the church at Corinth in A.D. 51, the Corinthian Christians were New Carnal Christians, new born babies in Christ. So Paul fed them with milk [gospel truths presented in a simple way], for they were not sufficiently developed to be able to eat meat [gospel truths presented in mature way]. Now six years later, the Corinthians had become Christians, yet

Old Carnal Christians who still need to be fed with milk, and not yet with meat. They had been given a full six years opportunity for growth and development. Paul blames them for being carnal Christians. Growth and development in Christ is vital. The Bible says that to be carnally minded is death, but to be spiritually minded is life and peace [Rom 8:5-8]. Every Christian must desire to grow spiritually. This does not happen overnight, but takes time and effort.

## The Old and New Nature

When one becomes a Christian he receives a new nature. *"Therefore if any man be in Christ, he is a new creature: old things are passed away; behold all things are become new"* [2Cor 5:17]. His old attributes do not vanish. The only difference is that a new character has been introduced, therefore he now possesses two natures, the old and the new. The new nature is received by the indwelling of the Holy Spirit when one is born again [Rom 8:9]. This nature brings transformations, expecting you to appreciate and obey its conditions. This is a challenge since the new Christian has been *"gratifying the craving of his sinful nature [his flesh] and following its desires and thoughts.'* [Eph 2:3 NIV].

Though the new nature brings transformations, these changes can materialize only if there is a breakthrough from the slavery of sin [Rom 6:16]. The old nature does not die, but needs to be suppressed until it is under control. As the Apostle Paul says, *"... I beat my body and make it my slave so that after I have preached to others, I myself will not be disqualified for the prize.'* [1 Cor 9:27 NIV]. It is necessary to exercise self-control and be master over your body, your thoughts and your actions. The moment you decide to disobey the new nature, the old nature takes over.

There is a struggle in you, and it is you who can determine who wins. Never give in to the appetites of your flesh, keep on resisting them. The secret of breaking through, lies in yielding, that is, you need to surrender yourself entirely to God and be led by the Holy Spirit. When in submission to the Holy Spirit, its ruling power will guard and fight for you. It's not you who live, but Christ lives in you. The life you live in the body, you live by faith in the Son of God [Gal 2:20]. This is the secret, not to give in to the demands of the enemy. The Holy Spirit is there to help you. Allow Him to guide you, he does not use force, he is waiting for you to give Him preference.

## Stages of a Christian Life

When someone is just born again he/she is excited about the new life, the newly found saviour and friend. After some time the excitement fades off. You may then start to feel as if you are not saved. It is not a matter of emotions or feelings, but faith. *".... If you confess with your mouth, 'Jesus is Lord,' and believe in your heart that God raised Him from the dead, you will be saved. For it is with your heart you believe and are justified, and it is with your mouth that you confess and are saved.'* [Romans 10:9-10 NIV]. Below are some stages a Christian can go through:

➢ **Excitement Stage.** Soon after salvation and baptism. The Christian is full of excitement, and is zealous for the Lord. He sits on the front bench and is active in all church activities. He asks questions, takes the word of God seriously, and actively seeks to change for good.

➢ **Fighting Stage.** The struggle of the old and the new nature starts to happen. The old patterns try to come back, due to seemingly good reasons.

➢ **Hesitant Stage.** When excitement dies off and one is faced with temptations. He now sits in the crowd and now behaves like everyone else. The Christian prefers to be average and judges himself against other Christians. He is easily swayed by any wind of doctrines [Eph 4:14].

➢ **Truth Confusion Stage.** He is in need of the truth of the Word of God as he is faced with many challenges as well as false doctrines and philosophies. He is easily attracted by false religions.

➢ **Dormant Stage.** This is the time when he has settled down spiritually. He thinks he is grown and knows many things. Then he starts to relax, relying on his own knowledge, theory and experience. Outwardly he seems spiritual, but inside there is nothing. He becomes a back bencher.

Time is also an important factor in developing your Christian life. There are no short cuts. The more time one takes to build, the deeper and stronger the spiritual life. When God wants to make an oak tree, He takes 100 years, but when He wants to make a squash, He takes six months.

## Beware of These challenges

The devil sets up snares for Christians. Listed below are some of the traps which he uses to hook unsuspecting believers. These are some of the weapons he uses, *"for we are not unaware of his schemes."* [2 Cor 2:11 NIV].

i.  **Desires of the World** - Be absorbed into the world's systems [1 John 2:15]:
    - A material blessing the world offers becomes a central desire.
    - Honour and recognition by people becomes the goal.
    - Feeling secure and comfortable with those of the world.
ii.  **Desire of the flesh and Old sins** – The Devil exploit your weakest points or habits e.g. alcohol, smoking, sexual addictions [Rom 6:6-14, 12:1-2].
iii.  **Bad friends – [Amos 3:3]**
    - Yoked with unbeliever [2 Cor 6:14, 7:1].
    - Bad company [1 Cor 15:33, 2 Thess 3:6-14].
    - Being ineffective [Matt 5:13-16].
iv.  **Worldliness [Jam 5:5, 1 John 2:15-17]**
    - Amusement in form of being closely engrossed by secular music, movies, literature etc.
    - Love of fashion and money [1 Tim 6:10, 2 Tim 3:1-5].
v.  **Customs and cultural practices**
    - Some religious practices.
    - Some cultural or even occult practices
vi.  **Lack of commitment**
    - Absent from fellowship meetings [Heb 10:24-25].
    - Failure to support church activities.
    - Failure to study the word or pray [Deut 17:19, Josh 1:8].
    - Failure to tell others about Jesus.
vii.  **Spirituality** – 'sinless perfection' and pride.
    - Too reserved and isolated
    - Too big to ask for forgiveness from God.

### Advice for Daily Victorious Living

To avoid falling into some of these pits, below are some tips for daily living:

- ✓ Confess and forsake all known sins – 1John 4:9.
- ✓ Live a clean life – Ps 1:1-3, Josh 1:8
- ✓ Walk in step with the Holy Spirit – Eph 5:18, Gal 5:16.
- ✓ Recognise temptation is not a sin, yielding to it is the sin – James 1:13-15.
- ✓ There is a way of escape – 1 Cor 10:13, James 4:7.
- ✓ Keep the right focus and priorities in life – Col 3:1-2, Phil 4:8.
- ✓ Keep away from obvious areas of temptations – Ps 101:3.
- ✓ Be aware of Satan's schemes – 2 Cor 2:11.

A victorious Christian life is not 'a stroll in the park.' Satan will try again and again to put challenges across your path. Jesus reassured us in John 16:33 that because he overcame, we can overcome as well. Your victory has been assured, so hang on to the one who assured your victory. Keep a healthy relationship with God, so that you can overcome.

# 3. WHO IS GOD?

God [*theos* in Greek] is Lord, that is, *'I am who I am'* [Ex 3:14 NIV]. Lord means Yahweh [*YHWH* in Hebrew] is the divine name of God and is called LORD in capital letters. This is the almighty God, the Supreme Being, the divine Creator, the Master of the universe [heavens and earth]. He is the God of all mankind, the only one true God.

## The Existence of God
The existence of God is never argued in the Bible. Genesis 1:1 began by saying, *"In the beginning God created the heaven and the earth."* It assumes that all men know that God exists. Why then that assumption? The existence of God is the primary [first] truth, a perception of moral reason. Common sense tells us there is a God. This primary truth is not written upon the human mind at birth, but it is a truth that is known as we observe, reflect and reason concerning nature. *"The fool says in his heart, 'there is no God'"* [Ps 53:1 NIV].

By rational argument we see the well designed, and orderly arranged world. Think of your existence and the existence of all things. There certainly is the designer and architect. Where is the origin? Can the creation of a human being like you just come from an ape? You have intellect, sensibility and a will. There is definitely a perfect Creator.

Due to our human nature of seeking for truth and fulfilment, men become aware of the existence of God. No race or tribe in any place of the earth has no knowledge of God's existence. But unfortunately surprisingly, some men reject the existence of God. No man is born an atheist but becomes one. There is a God in heaven!

## Existing Beliefs of God
*Atheism* teaches that God does not exist. *Agnosticism* teaches that existence of God cannot be known. *Pantheism* teaches that God is everything and everything is God. *Polytheism* teaches that there are many gods. *Deism* teaches that God made the universe and withdrew from the universe, leaving it to run on its own. *Theism* teaches that there is one God who is supreme over all creation, but yet immanent in the universe. This is the true view of God. Whether you choose to believe that God is there or not, God remains God. All other gods are inventions made by man, lies that pretend, vanities

that are useless, and gods newly come up [Ps 40:4, 106:29, Exodus 20:3, Deut 32 :17].

## Some Attributes of God

God's attributes are His character, His divine excellence, His revelation of His mysterious essence. God's glory is the sum of His attributes.

- God is infinitely wise – Rom 16:27, 1 Tim 1:17
- God is Spirit – John 4:23-24
- God is life – Matt 5:48
- God is unique – Isaiah 40:25
- God is eternal – Psalm 90:2
- God is omniscient [all-knowing] – Job 36:4, 37:16
- God is omnipotent [all powerful]. Nothing is too hard for Him – Gen 18:14, Matt 19:26
- God is Holy in essence, thoughts, words and deeds. He is separated from evil – Isa 6:3, 1 Peter 1:16
- God is love. His love for all of His creation – John 3:16, 1 John 4:8
- God is just and righteous. He is right in all His dealings – Gen 18:25
- God is merciful and good. He often withholds punishment from rebellious people – Exodus 34:6, Psalm 23:6, Rom 2:3-6
- Self-existence; He is uncaused and independent – Isa 43:10, John 5:26
- Immutability; God is unchangeable – Num 23:19, Mal 3:6, James 1:17
- Infinity; Apart from being omnipresent [present everywhere], God is also free from all limitations. He is not limited in perfection, time and space.

## God Reveals Himself

You cannot discover God apart from His self-revelation [Job 11:7]. *"Because that which may be known of God is manifest in them; for God hath shewed it unto them. For the invisible things of him from the creation of the world are clearly seen, being understood by the things that are made, even his eternal power and Godhead; so that they are without excuse"* [Rom 1:19-20]. It is God who discloses himself to man. God shows himself to man through:

a) **Natural Revelation.** It is general revelation of indirect revelation given to man by God through the medium of creation. We can know more about the creator through his creation. *"The heavens declare the glory of God; the skies proclaim the works of his hands. Day after day they pour forth speech; night after night they display knowledge. Their voice goes out into all the earth, their words to the end of the world. In the heavens has pitched a tent for the sun, which is like a bridegroom coming forth from his pavilion, like a champion rejoicing to run his* course. It rises at one end of the heavens and makes his circuit to the other; nothing is hidden from its heat." [Ps 19:1-6 NIV]. Through our conscience and through history, God also reveals himself to men. But natural revelation is limited. It does not tell us of things like God's provision and salvation. It is blurred since man is under a curse. Sometimes it is ignored especially by today's people who are so much involved in worldly affairs.

b) **Supernatural Revelation.** It is special or direct revelation given immediately from God to man. This can be through dreams, visions [Num 12:6], angels, face to face revelations [Gen 12:7], the Holy Spirit and Jesus Christ [Heb 1:1-2]. Much of the supernatural revelation is recorded in the Bible. This is then taught to all people so that they may have the knowledge of God. The Bible is the inscribed supernaturally revealed Word of God.

c) **Jesus Christ.** Man was made in the image of God. He was perfect and sinless in conduct. His purpose was to reflect God's glory to all creation, thereby revealing God to the whole creation. But when man fell, he was now biased towards sin, therefore he could not clearly reveal God. God had to send his son Jesus to reveal himself. Jesus Christ is a human revelation of God [John 1:18, Col 1:15-20]. God spoke to us through his son. It is through Him that God created the universe. Jesus reflects the brightness of God's glory and is the exact representation of God's own being [Heb 1:1-3]. Jesus came as 'God manifest in flesh' or as 'God with us.' Through Him the nature of God was made known to the world [1 John 1:1-2].

All of the three ways of revelations are important. God speak to us through all these means.

## The Revealed Names of God
God has three supreme names:
1. **"Elohim":** It is translated as 'God' in King James Version [KJV]. It means God the creator. It emphasizes God's power, sovereignty, rule and pre-eminence of God. Elohim is also used in reference to false gods as well as the true God. The chief combination names are:
   i. El Shaddai – the mighty God [Gen 17;1].
   ii. El Elyon – the most high God [Gen 14:18].
   iii. El Roi – God who sees [Gen 16:13].
   iv. El Olam – everlasting or eternal God [Gen 21:33, Isa 40:28].

2. **"Jehovah"**: It is translated as 'Lord' in KJV. It means the redeemer, and emphasizes God's self-existence, eternity and covenant faithfulness. Jehovah is a name applied only to the true God. The main combination names are:
   i. Jehovah Jireh – the Lord who provides [Gen 22:14].
   ii. Jehovah Rohi – the Lord our shepherd [Ps23:1].
   iii. Jehovah Ropheka/Rapha – the Lord our physician [Ex 15:26].
   iv. Jehovah Tsidkenu – the Lord our righteousness [Jer 23:6].
   v. Jehovah Shalom – the Lord our peace [Judge 6:24].
   vi. Jehovah Nissi – the Lord my banner [Ex 17:15].
   vii. Jehovah Shammah – the Lord is present [Ezekiel 48:25].
   viii. Jehovah Maccaddeschem – the Lord our sanctifier, or who make you holy [Ex 31:13, Lev 20:8].
   ix. Jehovah Zebaoth/Sabbaoth – the Lord of hosts [Hag 1:2, 9, Zech 1:3]. This is the chief name used by Jews after their return from exile. It is used often by Jeremiah, Haggai and Malachi.
3. **"Adonai"**: It is translated as 'Lord' in KJV. It means the Master, and emphasizes the Lordship, authority and position of God. It is used to reference men as masters [Ps 68:32, Isa 6:8-11].

"Jehovah Elohim" – the 'Lord God' is a combination of two chief names of God, referring Him as both Redeemer and Creator. All the names of God are a revelation of his attributes [characteristics].

**The Trinity of God**
There is but one God who dwells in and manifests Himself through three divine equal persons, the Father, the Son and the Holy Spirit. All three of whom are united in one Godhead, and all three of whom are called "God" because they share the same God-character.

The trinity cannot be known apart from supernatural revelation. It is revealed in both the Old and New Testament:
➢ Gen 1:1-2: 'God' and the Holy Spirit are mentioned.
➢ Gen 1:26, 11:7: God says 'Let us' which is plural.
➢ Isa 6:3: The words, Holy, Holy, Holy' indicate the tri-personality.
➢ Matt 3:16-17: At the baptism of Christ, the three persons are mentioned.
➢ Matt 28:19: In the great commission, the trinity is mentioned.
➢ John 6:27, 10:29: The Father is called God.
➢ Heb 1:8, John 1:1, 14:9-10: The Son is declared God.
➢ Acts 5:3-4: The Holy Spirit is called God.
➢ 1 Cor 12:4-6: The trinity is mentioned.

➢ 2 Cor 13:14: Again the three members mentioned.
➢ Rev 1:4-5: The message to the seven churches of Asia is from the three members of the Godhead.

## The Work of the Trinity

- The Father plans, the Son executes and the Holy Spirit applies.
- The Father sends the Son [John 12:44, Gal 4:4], and the Father and the Son send the Holy Spirit [John 14:26, 16:7]. The Son never sends the Father, nor does the Holy Spirit ever send the Father or the Son.

The word trinity is not in the Bible. Tertullian [A.D. 150 – 230], a church leader of North Africa was the first to use the term 'trinity' and formulate the teaching of the trinity. The doctrine was refined by the council of Nicea, in A.D. 325, and was perfected by Augustine around A.D. 400. *"Hear, O Israel: The Lord our God is one Lord"* [Deut 6:4]. There is only one true God.

# 4. THE WORD OF GOD

## The Bible
The Bible [*Biblos* in Greek] is simply the Book of books, and the written Word of God. The central purpose and theme is 'God's loving plan to rescue mankind' [2 Tim 3:15-16]. It contains 66 books that are divided basically the Old and New Testament.

The Old Testament has 39 books that are classified as:
- o **17 Historical books** (Genesis to Esther) of which the first five books are called the 'Pentateuch' [five scrolls].
- o **5 Poetry and Wisdom books** (Job to Song of Solomon).
- o **17 Prophetical books** (Isaiah to Malachi) which are divided into;
  - a) 5 Major Prophets (Isaiah to Daniel) and.
  - b) 12 Minor Prophets (Hosea to Malachi).

The New Testament has 27 books which are classified as:
- o **4 Gospel books** (Matthew to John).
- o **1 Historical book** (Acts).
- o **21 Doctrinal books** (Romans to Jude). These are sometimes called the letters or Epistles.
- o **1 Prophetic book** (Revelations).

## Who Wrote the Bible?
**The Divine Author** –The Bible comes from God through the divine inspiration of the Holy Spirit [2 Tim 3:16, 2 Peter 1:21]. There are many more evidences to support this claim.

**The Human Authors** – The Bible came from God through the divine inspiration of the Holy Spirit through the Human agency of God – chosen men. The 66 books were written by up to 40 human authors, coming from all walks of life. Some were kings, others were priests, others were prophets, others were farmers, others were herdsmen, others were fishermen, one was a tax collector, one was a physician, etc. They wrote over a period of around 1600 years and independently of each other.

## Who Was the Bible Written For?

The 39 books of the Old Testament are addressed directly to the physical descendants of Abraham, the Israelites, and the 27 books of the New Testament are addressed directly to the spiritual descendants of Abraham, the church. Indirectly, the Bible is addressed to all men [Rom 15:4]. The Bible is for ordinary people, not Christians only. It is not written in a secret code, which needs to be cracked for its message to be understood. The decisive qualifications for profitable Bible study are spiritual rather than intellectual. The Bible is relevant. Its aim is to change the life of the reader, as well as to capture his aesthetic interest, and supply him with historical and theological information. God himself does not change, in nature or his dealings with men. Therefore the message of the Bible is for us. Jesus Christ the personal Word of God, is both divine and human, so is the Bible. These are some of the names given to the Bible: the (Holy) Scriptures [the writings], the Word of God, the Divine Library [the Bibliotheca Divina] or the Book(s).

## Logos and Rhema

The word of God can be either Rhema or Logos. The Rhema word of God is the living, life giving, and active word of God. It is also called the empowered Word of God, which speaks to the current situation. This word produces results, and is enforced by the Holy Spirit. The Logos Word of Gods is the written or inscriptive Word of God. This is the word in the Bible. The examples below from the Bible will help to differentiate the two:

- *"But he answered and said, It is written (Logos), Man shall not live by bread alone, but by every word (Rhema) that proceedeth out of the mouth of God."* [Matt 4:4].
- *"These were more noble than those in Thessalonica, in that they received the word (Rhema) with all readiness of mind, and searched the scriptures (Logos) daily, whether those things were so."* [Acts 17:11].
- *"So then faith cometh by hearing, and hearing by the word (Rhema) of God."* [Rom 10:17].
- *"Jesus answered and said unto them, Ye do err, not knowing the scriptures (Logos), nor the power of God (Rhema)"* [Matt 22:29].

You must know the scripture (Logos) in order to judge whether the Word (Rhema) is from God. The Holy Spirit (Rhema) and the Holy Bible (Logos) always agree. It is the Rhema component which comes to us as we read the Bible that transforms us, whilst the Logos is captured by our minds. When Jesus was on earth his words were Rhema [John 6:63]. And He himself is the Rhema word of God [John 1:1-18].

As you read the Bible, allow the Holy Spirit to enlighten the scriptures so that they become the Rhema word, addressing your current situation.

## The Word of God
- Points people to Jesus – John 20:30-31.
- Builds a relationship with God – 1 Peter 1:23.
- Equips us for battle – Eph 6:17.
- Guides our conduct – 1 Tim 1:18-19.
- Produces life – John 6:23, and is creative – Ps 33:6-9, Heb 11:3.
- Is pure and without error Pro 30:5.
- Cleanse us like water – John 15:3, Eph 5:25-27.
- Keep us clean – Ps 119:9, 11.
- Is light to our lives – Ps 19:8, Ps 119:105.
- Is spiritual food – Matt 4:4, 1 Cor 3:1-2.
- Is like a sword – Heb 4:12.
- Helps us to pray – John 15:7.

## Know the Word Personally
*"By the word of the Lord heavens were made, and all the host of them by the breath of his mouth"* [Ps 33:6]. *"… the words were framed by the word of God,"* [Heb 11:3]. We have seen that the Bible is God's word, therefore we are commanded to read it [Josh 1:8].

**Read it often:** The more we read God's word, the more familiar it becomes. In this way it changes us as our faith grows, and we become more like Jesus (the word that became flesh – John 1:14). His word will have a better effect upon our feeling and our actions. We will enjoy both the grace of God and the beauty of God [Ps 119:103, Jer 15:16]. If carefully translated, any translation cannot reduce the qualities of God's word. Knowing God's word means more than just reading it.

**Study to Understand:** The study of the word of God should be regular, open minded and concentrated. We can then learn about God, man and their relationship [Ps 19:8, Ps 119:104-106]. We can realize our part and responsibility in His plan. We can believe His message and we can act upon it [John 5:39, Acts 17:11]. Study helps to grow in understanding [1 Peter 2:2, 2 Peter 3:18]. This enables us to worship, live, be faithful and fruitful.

**Memorise:** Our memories grow stronger as we use them more frequently. This helps us to know God's word [Ps 119:11, Col 3:16] and apply it in times of need. Jesus had memorized the word so *"he answered and said, it is written 'man shall not live by bread alone, but by every word that proceeds from the mouth of God'"* [Matt 4:4].

## The Influence of the Bible

As we have already discovered, the Bible contains supernatural revelation. Natural revelation is revelation of the truths of God revealed through: (1) created things; (2) conscience; and (3) history. Supernatural (special) revelation is revelation of truths of God, revealed through direct revelation from God.

No other book has so greatly influenced the nations and the individuals of the world, as has the Bible. It has had tremendous influence upon the nations and the people of Western Civilization. For instance, the great majority of the more than 35 million laws on the statute books of the world are based upon the "Ten Commandments" and the ethical teaching of Jesus. That's why Queen Victoria once said, "The Bible is the secret of England's greatness." Amen.

# 5. MANKIND AND SATAN

In this section we will look at two personalities that have been in conflict for ages, man and Satan. Who is man? Where did humanity originate from? What is the purpose of our existence? And where are we going? We will also look at Satan; his origin and his destiny.

## Mankind
Man's creation was long after creation of angels, around 6000 years ago. He was created by God Himself [Gen 1:26-27]. He was created in the image of God. Both God and man possess these three elements; (1) intellect (self-consciousness, ability to say I exist), (2) sensibility (moral consciousness, ability to say I ought), and (3) will (self-determination, ability to say I choose). He was created in God's likeness; inclined to God, with moral purity and holiness like that of God. He was full of the Holy Spirit, was in fellowship with God and was happy and blessed.

But when man fell the three elements were not removed, but the intellect became darkened (filled with error); the senses were depraved (dominated by evil desires) and the will was weakened (weak to obey God). The Holy Spirit departed from him, the blessing turned into a curse, and man was filled with sorrow. His original attributes were also lost. Fortunately man can be restored if the above three are corrected, made right. The question now is how?

## Need for Salvation
When Adam sinned two things happened. Firstly, Adam's sin, and its penal consequence, was judicially imputed by God to him and his succeeding generations. Hence man was sentenced to death. Secondly, Adam's corrupted nature was transmitted to his offspring again. Man needs to be restored to his God. This is not possible as long as man is in a state of sin. A mediator was necessary to reconcile sinful man and a Holy God. So God "gave his only begotten Son, that whosoever believeth in him should not perish, but have everlasting life." [John 3:16]. God's provision of imputed righteousness for repentant sinners, is through the death of Jesus Christ. Jesus is the only way to God. Jesus is the only one who can save man from the curse of sin and death. He is our hope. "Jesus saith unto him, I am the way, the truth, and the life: no man cometh unto the Father, but by me." [John 14:6].

**How can Jesus save us?** The Bible clearly says that, *"if you confess with your mouth 'Jesus is Lord,' and believe in your heart that God raised him from the dead, you will be saved. For it is with your heart that you believe and are justified, and it is with your mouth that you confess and are saved"* [Rom 10:9-10 NIV]. This is the only way to be saved [1 John 1:9].

## What is Man's Purpose?

❖ That he might have dominion over the earth [Gen 1:28]. The blessing of God was intended to make him increase in everything, thereby the ability to rule over every creature.

❖ That he might reflect God's glory to the whole of creation [1 Cor 11:7, 1 Peter 2:9]. By being made in his image man is able to echo the splendour, the magnificence, the richness and the brilliance of his God and Father.

❖ That he might someday, after elevation to immortality have dominion over the whole creation [Ps 8, Heb 2:6-8]. This happens when man's body has been transformed.

## Who is Satan?

Satan is the master deceiver. He has so far deceived the world's billions of people to believe that he does not exist. He has covered his true identity even to those who believe that he exists, to the point of thinking of him as a monster or something preachers use to scare people to repent. Some think of him as a myth or evil spell. Others think he is a goblin or a joke to make fun of.

Satan is real. He is a being with intellect, sensibility and will. He thinks, knows, desires, hates, speaks etc [Matt 4:1-11, Gen 3:1]. He is a supernatural being. Like all angels, he has no physical body and not subjected to laws of nature. He is also normal with all norms of personality, but his intentions are evil.

## History of Satan

Ezekiel 28 provides us with most information on Satan. He is a created being, created by God and was anointed by God as a guardian angel. He was full of wisdom, perfect in beauty, anointed with authority, sinless in conduct. He was cast out of heaven after sinning [Luke 10:18. The causes of his fall are pride, selfish ambition and the *"I will"* [Isa 14:12-14]:

- Ascend into heaven,
- Be exalted above the stars of God,
- Sit upon the mount of congregation, in the sides of the north,
- Ascend above the heights of the clouds, and
- Be like the most high.

## Results of his fall
He is now 'Satan' and not 'Lucifer.' Lucifer means angel of light, while Satan means the opponent. He was left with wisdom but corrupted. His sin was the first, thereby becoming the first sinner. He was condemned and sentenced to be destroyed. No grace is available for him. He was cast from the mountain of God. He is cursed by God and is now the enemy of Man [Gen 3:14].

## Names of Satan
In heaven before his fall, he was called Lucifer, which means angels of light, [Isa 4:12] but he is now called:
- Satan (the opponent) – 1 Chron 21:1, Job 1:6.
- The Serpent or old serpent – Gen 3:1-4, Rev 12:9.
- The Deceiver – Rev 12:9; the Tempter – Matt 4:3, 1 The 3:5.
- The Dragon, serpent, devil, Satan – Rev 12:9, 20:2.
- The Devil (false accuser) – Matt 4:1-8, Eph 6:11-12, Rev 12:9.
- The evil one, the wolf – Matt 13:19, John 10:12.
- Beelzebub (dung-god) – Matt 12:24, Mark 14:19.
- The Adversary, the devil (enemy) – 1 Peter 5:8.
- The Murderer, the liar – John 8:44.
- The Prince of this world – John 12:31, 14:31, 16:11.
- The Accuser of our brethren – Rev 12:10.

## His Mission
1. To weaken and destroy God's kingdom – John10:10.
2. To strengthen and establish his own kingdom.

## His Weaknesses
1. He is limited by God. He has no power or authority over God – 1 King 22:19-22, Job 1:12, Rev 12:7-9.
2. He is limited by the believer. Man was given authority over Satan, if we resist him he flees – James 4:7, Gen 1:28.

Jesus came to destroy Satan's works [Heb 2:14, 1 John 3:8]. Satan has no power over Jesus [John 14:30]. Greater is Jesus in us than Satan in the world [1 John 4:4]. His authority was stripped through the cross [Col 2:15].

As we walk with Jesus, the power working in Him will start to work in our lives as well; bringing victory over all the afflictions that Satan throws at us. Born again Christians have absolute authority over Satan and his demons. You are more than a conqueror! [Rom 8:38].

# 6. WHO IS JESUS CHRIST?

Jesus (Joshua) means 'the salvation of Yahweh' or 'the Lord saves.' Christ, the official title of Jesus means 'the anointed one.' Christ is the Greek name used in the New Testament, while the Old Testament, which was written in Hebrew, uses 'the messiah' for Christ. The term 'Messiah' was commonly used after Malachi and before Jesus came, for the great King of whom the prophets spoke. The expectation of the coming Messiah grew stronger and stronger between the Old and the New Testaments.

## The Old Testament Points Towards Jesus
The Old Testament speaks of the coming Messiah in many places through direct and indirect prophecies:

I.  **Direct Prophecies:** Many verses in the books of the prophets [Isaiah to Malachi] speak of Christ. These prophecies show that the Messiah would be more than a human being [Isa 9:6-7, 53:1-12]. This made the expectation grow that the perfect King would come. He is often called a descendant of David [Amos 9:11, Isa 11:1]. The New Testament confirms that these prophecies talk of Jesus Christ [Luke 24:27, 44].

II. **Indirect Prophecies:** The New Testament [e.g. the gospel of Matthew] uses many references from the Old Testament when speaking of Jesus. All these prophecies show that Jesus is the one and only saviour. No one can know God except through Jesus [John 14:6-9].

Jesus was called the Christ because he was the one whom God chose and sent as Saviour and Lord. Jesus Christ is part of the Godhead, that is, the Father, the Son and the Holy Spirit. He is the centre and purpose of God's revelation [Heb 1:1-13]. Without Christ the Old Testament is incomplete. The Old Testament prepared the world for accepting God's Son Jesus Christ, but many still did not accept him. Jesus was miraculously conceived by the Holy Spirit and born of Mary in 5 B.C. [Matt 2:13-15]. With God's grace upon Him, Jesus lived in Nazareth where he grew up in wisdom [mentally], in stature [physically], in favour with God [spiritually] and man [socially] [Luke 2:52]. He began His public ministry when he was 31 years old after the mission of John the Baptist.

## Purpose of His Coming
- To bridge the gap between God and man, that is, reconciling man to God [1 Tim 2:5].
- To reveal God to man by His life. Only Jesus is the one who came from heaven and can show man the attributes of God [Matt 11:27, John 1:18].
- To qualify Himself to be a merciful compassionate high priest by His suffering. He is the high priest who has been to heaven. For He is a priest in the order of Melchizedek [Heb 2:16-18, 4:15-16].
- To rescue mankind from Satan's power [Luke 19:10, Col 1:13].
- To give His life as a price to buy us back to God [Matt 20:28, John 3:16].
- To destroy the works of Satan in our lives [1 John 3:8].
- To give eternal life [1 John 5:11-12, John 3:16-17, John10:10].
- To give us new birth into the family of God [John 1:17, 1 John 3:1-3].
- To restore our fellowship with God the Father. This was done by the reconciling work of Christ [Rom 5:10].

## The Excellence of His Life
He lived a sinless life. Since He was born of God He had no sin in Him, and He never committed any sin [2 Cor 5:21, Heb 4:15]. Jesus delighted to do the will of the Father. His obedience was seen by His agonizing death on the cross [Matt 26:39, John 4:34]. His earthly life was a life of prayer, and He trusted God in everything [Mark 1:35, John 11:41-42]. Humility was one of His distinctions. Though He was God He chose to leave His glory, and to live as a servant to man. He suffered and died on the cross [in His first advent]. But when He comes again in His second advent, He is coming to conquer and reign [Rev 19:11-20].

## His Death
When Jesus had finished the Last Supper with His disciples, they went out to pray. This is where they met their enemies and Jesus was arrested. He was put through a trial that appeared to have broken all the appropriate legal rules. When the witness failed to produce sufficient evidence to condemn Him, He was forced to make, what His judges regarded as the blasphemous statement (to Christians it was the simple truth) that He was the Messiah. The Jews handed Him over to the Roman governor as a political rebel against Rome, and although the governor was privately convinced of His innocence, He allowed Him to be put to death by the Roman punishment of crucifixion. However, God had a more excellent plan for the redemption of all mankind. Jesus' death had these features:

- It was a voluntary death [John 10:17-18]. He did not die as a victim or a martyr, but as a voluntary sacrifice. Because of His love for us, He came to save us by sacrificing His life.
- It was a substitutive death on behalf of sinners. The wages of sin is death. All man sinned, so they deserved death, but He took upon himself our sins as well as our punishment [Rom 6:23].
- It was a reconciling death. God reconciled to mankind [2 Cor 5:19].
- He died on the cross for us [1 Peter 2:24, Isa 53:5-6].

After three days in the tomb, God raised His son Jesus from the dead [Eph 2:4-6]. Jesus opened the door of heaven for us to follow. He ascended to heaven 40 days after His resurrection, from mount Olives (the place to which He will return at His Second Advent) [Zech 14:14]. He ascended in a glory cloud i.e. shekinah glory cloud, coming down and receiving him. He was carried to heaven were He sat down at the right hand of the Father [Mark 16:19].

## Glorification of Christ
Firstly, restoration to Christ to His former glory [John 17:5], the Shekinah glory that He had before He came down to earth. Secondly, the bestowal upon Christ of new glory after the approval of His earthly work by the Father [John 13:32]. Because of His work that has been accomplished:
- God made Him "Lord" – Acts 2:36, Rom 14:9.
- God made Him "the Christ" – Acts 2:36, Heb1:9.
- God made Him "the First born" – Col 1:18, James 1:18.
- God made Him "Prince" – Acts 5:31, Ps 72:8-11.
- God made Him "Saviour" – Acts 5:31, Eph 5:23.
- God made Him "the High Priest" – Heb 5:5-6, Heb 4:14-16.
- God made Him "the Head of the church" – Eph 1:22-23.

Christians are believers in, or followers of Jesus Christ. They were first called Christians at Antioch [Acts 11:26]. This is because they imitated Christ, and followed His teachings. Should we follow other men? [1 Cor 3:3-9]. How can we become Christians? By believing in Jesus. Just as one man's (Adam) disobedience all were made sinners, so by one man's (Jesus Christ) obedience many will be called righteous. God gave His only son, thereby, reconciling man to Himself. He gave His only begotten son, by that sacrifice, He received many more sons. Jesus, the central man in the Bible is God's plan for the salvation of mankind.

# 7. THE CROSS AND THE BLOOD OF JESUS

*"'What shall I do, then with Jesus who is called Christ?' Pilate asked. They all answered, "crucify him!"'* [Mark 15:12-13 NIV]. When Jesus Christ was put to death by being nailed to a wooden cross, wicked men thought they were executing a man who was disturbing their way of life. They did not realize that the cross was planned by God.

At the end of his life, the man whom wise men from the east had called a content to worship was sold like a slave for thirty pieces of silver. Jesus got a royal robe and crown at last, but it was cruel and a mockery. He was scourged [Matt 27:26], then made to carry the cross to Golgotha (in Hebrew) or Calvary (in Latin) [both means a place of skull]. Blood from the wounds on his back clotted on the robe, and the crown of thorns streaked His face with more blood. He was stripped, and then nailed by hands and feet. He was left hanging in agony, as the Roman soldiers played dice and gambled for his clothes, until he died. This is the greatest crime in history, murdering the Son of the Almighty God.

## What is the Cross?
It was made from a tree [Acts 5:30] and alludes to the curse attached to a dead body hung on a tree. According to the Jewish law: *"And if a man have committed a sin worthy of death, and he be to be put to death, and thou hang him on a tree: His body shall not remain all night upon the tree,"* [Deut 21:22-23]. They made sure to bury him that day, because anyone who is hung on a tree is cursed. So the cross is a curse and the hanging person is cursed. Jesus freed us from the curse of sin by Him becoming a curse. In the same manner he restores to us the blessing of Abraham [Gal 3:13]. Jesus never liked the cross. He endured it for us.

There are many crosses, but the cross of Jesus Christ is the cross of redemption. How can it be redemptive? It carried a man who never sinned, a man who exchanged his holiness for our cursed sins. Just as he was still on the cross, the power of His cross began to manifest, shown by the fact that the thief gave his life to Christ on the cross. The thief was heading for hell, but he saw the cross of redemption, the cross of Christ. This is the cross that can save us. This is the cross that you need. Being sorry for your sins is not good enough. It won't save you. Sin dwells in the soul. It is a like cancer. You can't just forget your cancer and expect it to be cured. It is only through the cross that you can be saved.

It is a fact that:
- Jesus died in place of every individual in the world – 1 John 2:2.
- Jesus took the punishment for our sins on the cross – Isa 53:5-6.
- God removed our sorrows on the cross – Isa 53:4.
- God revealed His power through the cross – 1 Cor 1:18.
- God shows His love on the cross – Rom 5:8.

## Reconciliation Through The Cross

The cross made it possible for us to know God personally, to experience his love, peace and joy. We became acceptable to God through the cross. *"Therefore if any man is in Christ, he is a new creature: old things are passed away; behold all things are become new. And all things are of God, who has reconciled us to himself by Jesus Christ, and has given to us the ministry of reconciliation. To which, that God was in Christ, reconciling the world to himself, not imputing their trespasses unto them; and has committed unto us the word of reconciliation. Now then we are ambassadors for Christ, as though God did beseech you by us: we pray you in Christ's stead, you to be reconciled to God. For he has made him to be sin for us, who knew no sin; that we might be made the righteousness of God in him"* [2 Cor 5:17-21]. We receive forgiveness through the cross and become members of God's family through the cross. Racial barriers are broken through the cross. Therefore there is no Jew or Greek, no black or white, no male or female. We are all the same in Christ.

## The Blood of Jesus

It is also called the blood of Christ His Son [1 John1:7], the blood of his cross [Col 1:20], the blood of the Lord [1 Cor 11:27], the innocent blood [Matt 27:4], the precious blood [1 Peter 1:19] or the blood of the Lamb [Rev 7:14, 12:11]. This is the blood that was shed on the cross of Calvary.

There is life in the blood of animals. *"For the life of the flesh is in the blood: and I have given it to you upon the altar to make an atonement for your souls: for it is the blood that maketh an atonement for the soul."* [Lev 17:11]. Remove the blood from an animal, then it will die. When we sin, we deserve death [Rom 6:23]. Now Jesus paid this penalty of sin by shedding his blood. The blood of animals (just like that of babies) is innocent. It was used to cover sins. Day after day, every priest stands and performs his religious duties; again and again, he offers the same sacrifices, which can never take away sins. The blood of goats and bulls on those who are ceremonially unclean sanctify them so that they are outwardly clean.

But the blood of Jesus is more than just innocent. It is blameless and pure, therefore it can remove our sins. It is Christ who was sacrificed once and for all to take the sins of many people by bearing their sins. He gave his life (shed his blood) on the cross for our atonement. *"And without shedding of blood is no remission"* [Heb 9:22].

## Benefits from the Blood

Sin separates us from God, just as the Prophet Isaiah said, *"Behold, the LORD'S hand is not shortened, that it cannot save; neither his ear heavy, that it cannot hear: But your iniquities have separated between you and your God, and your sins have hid his face from you, that he will not hear. For your hands are defiled with blood, and your fingers with iniquity; your lips have spoken lies, your tongue hath muttered perverseness."* [Isa 59:1-3].

Because of our transgression we are guilty. It allows Satan to accuse us. But if we are without blemish, there is no condemnation. The devil cannot capitalize on our sins and accuse us, for he is the accuser of brethren. Sin demands the death penalty. *"Behold, all souls are mine; as the soul of the father, so also the soul of the son is mine: the soul that sins, it shall die"* [Ezekiel 18:4].

It is solely through the blood of Jesus that our fellowship with God is restored, that we are redeemed, (purchased back from slavery), that we are cleansed from guilt, that we are sanctified, that we are given boldness to enter God's presence, that we gain purity of heart and eternal life [Heb 9:22].

## The Power of the Blood

The blood puts God on man's side against the devil, and the devil has no ground for accusations [Rom 8:31-34]. The blood dissolves all Satan's legal rights of ownership [Col 1:14]. Redemption means to buy back, to compensate or to repay [Acts 20:28].

*"Forasmuch as ye know that ye were not redeemed with corruptible things, as silver and gold, from your vain conversation received by tradition from your fathers; But with the precious blood of Christ, as of a lamb without blemish and without spot"* [1 Peter 1:18-19]. Satan did and does not understand the cross. *"But we speak the wisdom of God in a mystery, even the hidden*

*wisdom, which God ordained before the world unto our glory: which none of the princes of the world knew: for had they known it, they would not have crucified the Lord of glory"* [1Cor 2:7-8]. In this case Satan is the prince and ruler of this age/world. This is God's secret wisdom revealed to us, which has been hidden from the wise and prudent, but has been revealed to babies, the revelation that had been hidden in God from the beginning of ages, the mystery of Christ.

The cross has power to redeem man and restore him to his divinely appointed place of authority. The blood and the cross provide all the protection against the forces of evil. The devil's power over our lives was broken at Calvary. Jesus "disarmed" and "dethroned" the devil on the cross. *"And having spoiled principalities and powers, he made a shew of them openly, triumphing over them in it"* [Col 2:15]. He stripped him off his power. Now the devil trembles. The authority was given to us such that, we have authority and legal right to tell the devil (and his demons) where to go and what to do. The reason the Son of God appeared was/is to destroy the work of the devil [1 John 3:8]. This happened on the cross of Calvary. There the divine mission was completed!

Destroy does not mean the devil no longer exists, but it means:
- Makes him powerless,
- Bring to naught,
- Reduce to zero i.e. nullified,
- Make of no effort,
- Disabled i.e. make inactive (deactivated).

That's what Paul said *"For I determined not to know anything among you, save Jesus Christ, and him crucified"* [1Cor 2:2]. His blood is the cost of our redemption, and so is His cross as to His love.

# 8. SALVATION

Salvation [*soterias* in Greek] in general means deliverance, pardon, liberation or redemption from danger or evil. In this section we will look at the salvation that was instituted through Christ's death on the cross. It involves deliverance from all that separates people from God. It can be from sin [Matt 1:21], the power of the devil [1 John 3:8], the effects of sin, or from the wrath of God [Matt 24:13]. In this lesson we will concentrate on deliverance from the guilt and power of sin. By his death and resurrection, Jesus brings salvation to people who believe in Him [John 3:16]. This salvation is basically restoration of man to the blessed state from which Adam fell, and elevation to the state that Adam would have attained had he not fallen i.e. the state of immorality and supremacy.

## What is Sin?
Sin simply the biblical word for failing to live up to God's standard. It includes meanings from 'error' to 'wickedness.' It can be sin of omission (failure to conform to God's Standards) or sin of commission (to commit a sin). Sin is not a list of categories of deeds or attitudes, but rather a condition. Man is by nature, a sinner. Therefore apart from imputed guilt of Adam's sinful nature, all men (who have reached the age of accountability) commit actions which are sinful [Rom 3:10-12, 1 John 1:8-10]. Man's sinful condition (a spiritual disease) has separated him from God, since God is holy and just, and must punish sin, therefore all men are in need of God's salvation.

## Who Can Save Man?
Christ is the saviour of men. He is the author and finisher of our faith [Heb 12:2]. Although He was/is God in the form of man, he took upon Himself the punishment and gave Himself as a sacrifice in our place, dying for our sins. This sacrificial death, and subsequent resurrection of Jesus from the dead, is sufficient penalty. We must then accept Christ's sacrificial death as having validity and meaning for us, if we repent and come to God by faith. He is faithful and just to forgive our sins and give us new nature and eternal life.

We are saved by grace through faith. It is not our own effort that can deliver us. Grace is the undeserving love of God, and favour towards people, because of the work of Jesus. Therefore:
- We are saved by the grace through faith – Rom 4:16, Gal 2:16.
- Not by works or sacraments – Rom 11:6, Eph 2:9.

- We believe through grace – Acts 18:27.
- Eternal life - Rom 5:21, Titus 3:7.
- Forgiveness of sin through grace – Eph 1:7.

## What is Repentance?

Repentance is turning from sin and self-centeredness towards God in order to trust, love and obey Him as Lord, the Supreme Being, the Master and King of your life. It is the first step we take to receive the salvation that God offers to us in the Lord Jesus Christ [Acts 2:36-38].

Repentance is not just feeling guilty. Feeling guilty is a God given indicator that shows that something is not right. Feeling guilty drives us to repent, but not all who feel guilty actually repent. In Acts 24:25 KJV, *"And as he (Paul) reasoned of righteousness, temperance, and judgment to come, Felix trembled, and answered, Go thy way for this time; when I have a convenient season, I will call for thee."* Felix felt guilty but did not repent. He knew that he should repent but he did not want to. You can feel guilty but choose to remain unrepentant.

Repentance is not just being sorry for your sin. Many people are sorry, not for what they have done wrong but for the penalty they receive in being caught. *"Now I rejoice, not that ye were made sorry, but that ye sorrowed to repentance: for ye were made sorry after a godly manner, that ye might receive damage by us in nothing. For godly sorrow worketh repentance to salvation not to be repented of: but the sorrow of the world worketh death."* [2 Cor 7:9-10]. It is not just trying to be a good person. Many people try in their own strength to become better and change their way of life. Self-effort leads to self-righteousness.

Repentance is not becoming religious. Even the Pharisees in the Bible fasted and prayed but never really repented. That's why Jesus said, *"For I say unto you, That except your righteousness shall exceed the righteousness of the scribes and Pharisees, ye shall in no case enter into the kingdom of heaven."* [Matt 5:20]. For the Pharisees were very religious but unrepentant. You can go to church; you can participate in all its activities and obey all its regulations for years without repenting. Repentance is not only knowing the truth. Knowledge of the truth does not mean that the truth has become a living reality in one's life. Having an intellectual knowledge of the truth does not help much, but the ability to apply the knowledge.

## True Repentance is:
- Being sorry to God for your sin – Ps 51:1-4.
- Being truthful about your sin – Ps 32:5.
- Turning away from your sin – Prov 28:13.
- Turning from yourself – 2 Cor 5:15.
- Turning from the devil – Acts 26:18.
- Turning to God – Zech 1:3.
- Turning to the right living – Rom 6:13.
- Turning from the world - 1 John 2:25.

## Blessedness of a Believer
*"Therefore if any man be in Christ, he is a new creature: old things are passed away; behold, all things are become new"* [2 Cor 5:17]. When we are born, we received the gift of eternal life. This is a step in our pilgrimage towards the state of supreme blessedness which we will have fully attained when our bodies are transformed. As in the book of Romans chapter eight, the stages are:

1. God elected us that is God acted first in order for us to turn to Him – Eph 1:4.
2. God foreknew us and predestined us – Rom 8:29, 11:2, Rom 8:29.
3. God called us [Rom 8:30] and invited us to accept salvation by faith, this is the general call of God.
4. God justified us [Rom 8:30]. This means that God can acquit (dismiss charges of) man of breaking his law, because the penalty has been paid through the death of Jesus Christ on cross.
5. God is sanctifying us [1 Cor 6:11]. This is the working of the Holy Spirit in the life of a believer, delivering him more and more from the power of the world, the flesh and the devil, and conforming him more and more into Christ likeness. This happens as a believer works out his salvation with fear and trembling.
6. God will glorify us [Rom 8:27, 8:30] this is an elevated state of perfection deserving and receiving praise and honour. This will happen when Christ calls us home. *"For our conversation is in heaven; from whence also we look for the Saviour, the Lord Jesus Christ: Who shall change our vile body, that it may be fashioned like unto his glorious body, according to the working whereby he is able even to subdue all things unto himself."* [Phil 3:20-21].

## Conversion

Conversion is changing belief, and has two sides; turning from sin in repentance, and turning to Christ, in faith. Turning from sin is called repentance, and turning to Christ is called faith. Repentance is always from sin and never of sin or for sin. Bible repentance is always an act of the will in the abandonment of sin. It is not leaving sin for some time due to some other reasons. Faith involves: (I) knowledge of Christ as Saviour, (ii) acknowledgement of Christ as Saviour, and (iii) adoption of Christ as Saviour. You now believe that Jesus Christ died for your sins, and only through him can we be forgiven. Are you saved? You need to be born again. Believe in Jesus, and you will be saved.

## Assurance of Salvation

Are you confident that you have eternal life, and that if you die today you will go to heaven? When one receives Jesus Christ as Saviour, it is not an emotional experience as such, but it is by faith. God wants you to know that you have eternal life. The Bible says, *"I write this to you who believe in (adhere to, trust in, and rely on) the name of the Son of God [in the peculiar services and blessings conferred by Him on men], so that you may know [with settled and absolute knowledge] that you [already] have life, yes, eternal life"* [1 John 5:13 Amp]. Jesus said, *"Verily, verily, I say unto you, He that believeth on me hath everlasting life"* [John 6:47]. It's Jesus who promised this. You have eternal life already because you believe in Him. Do not doubt your salvation. Jesus is now in your heart. If Satan tries to tell you that your sins have not yet been forgiven, resist him. Resist such kind of thoughts. When you act upon the word of God in faith, you can be sure of your salvation.

# 9. FAITH

The Greek word for faith is *Pistos*. *"Now faith is the substance of things hoped for, the evidence of things not seen"* [Heb 11:1]. It is the confident assurance that something we want is going to happen. It is to be sure of things we hope for. Simply, it is trust, dependence or reliance on God or the belief in His promises [Gen 15:5].

The faith that is discussed in Hebrew chapter eleven, is a lifelong posture of confident dependence on God's word. To have faith is to be certain about future things, the unseen realities. The Old Testament is full of examples of men and women who possessed a faith like this, who lived and died accordingly. And God was pleased with such men.

Faith comes from the word of God [Rom 10:17]. And without faith man cannot please or approach God [Heb 11:6]. Faith is a condition for salvation (forgiveness and eternal life) [Rom 10:10], and is also a quality that results from salvation [John 3:14-16, Gal 5:22]. True faith is (1) obedience and (2) action, in response to (3) hearing God's word (voice).

## Two Kinds of Knowledge
*"And my speech and my preaching was not with enticing words of man's wisdom, but in demonstration of the Spirit and of power: That your faith should not stand in the wisdom of men, but in the power of God. Howbeit we speak wisdom among them that are perfect: yet not the wisdom of this world, nor of the princes of this world, that come to nought: But we speak the wisdom of God in a mystery, even the hidden wisdom, which God ordained before the world unto our glory"* [1Cor 2:4-7]. Here the Bible talks of men's wisdom and God's secret wisdom.

i. **Sense Knowledge:** is all knowledge that comes to a natural man and come through the five senses [seeing, hearing, tasting, smelling and touching]. This is 'limited knowledge' called man's wisdom. As you preach or witness the word of God this is the audible component of the words. It makes the hearer understand the message logically.

ii. **Revelation Knowledge:** is not based on the five senses or natural reasoning, but on the truth of the God's Word. It is received through the spirit, that is, supernaturally, and is called God's wisdom. If you are preaching the word of God, this is the component of the Word that supernaturally goes deep inside, to touch the hearer's heart and communicate a message which no words can explain, thereby convicting the hearer. This type of knowledge comes through the power of the Holy Spirit.

## Basis of our Faith

i.  **The nature of God.** *"For when God made promise to Abraham, because he could swear by no greater, he sware by himself,"* [Heb 6:13]. He cannot change. *"For I am the Lord, I change not; therefore ye sons of Jacob are not consumed"* [Mal 3:6]. He cannot fail, and can do all things; none of his plans can be thwarted. He is a God who cannot lie. *"God is not a man, that he should lie; neither the son of man, that he should repent: hath he said, and shall he not do it? or hath he spoken, and shall he not make it good?"* [Num23:19]. He is a God who never forgets but remembers. *"For God is not unrighteous to forget your work and labour of love, which ye have showed toward His name, in that ye have ministered to the saints, and do minister"* [Heb 6:10].

ii. **Jesus our Saviour.** *"Looking unto Jesus the author and finisher of our faith; who for the joy that was set before him endured the cross, despising the shame, and is set down at the right hand of the throne of God"* [Heb 12:2]. Christ became the source of our faith. The fact of his death and resurrection provides ground for our believing. Jesus Christ has become for us wisdom from God, that is, our righteousness, holiness and redemption. It is through him that we can have anything. He said whatever you ask from the Father through me it will be done. He is the way, the truth and the life. We approach God through Jesus. He is the mediator and He is God.

iii. **The Word of God.** We depend on the word and promises of God. *"Heaven and earth shall pass away, but my words shall not pass away"* [Matt 24:35]. It is also written, *"Then said the Lord unto me, Thou hast well seen: for I will hasten my word to perform it"* [Jer 1:12]. The word of God does not return to him without accomplishing that which He has sent it to do. His Word stands true forever. His Word is powerful active and alive. It is his Word that made all creation into being. Faith comes when God brings a specific word, out of all he ever said, directly to us, realizing our faith. We depend on his Word.

## Faith that Grows

In Mark 6:5-6 the Amplified Bible says, *"And He was not able to do even one work of power there, except that He laid His hands on a few sickly people [and] cured them. And He marvelled because of their [corporate, combined] unbelief (their lack of faith in Him). And He went about among the surrounding villages and continued teaching."* If we join up in faith, great things will happen, and if we unite in unbelief, no great works happen. Therefore in verse 6 Jesus went about their villages teaching the Word of God. Why, because teaching the Word of God is the cure for unbelief. Remember, *"Faith comes by hearing and hearing by the word of God."* He called the twelve and sent them to preach. Verse 13 says, *"And they drove out many unclean spirits and anointed with oil many who were sick and cured them."* Miracles happened because they believed. They believed because they heard the Word of God.

Faith grows in stages. When the disciples asked Jesus to increase their faith, he answered, *"And the Lord said, If ye had faith as a grain of mustard seed, ye might say unto this Sycamine tree, Be thou plucked up by the root, and be thou planted in the sea; and it should obey you"* [Luke 17:6]. When we can't make a scripture work, we should not 'spiritualise' it. But God says in Jeremiah 1:12, *"for I will hasten my word to perform it."* Does little faith do big things? Little faith can only do little things. And big faith can do big things.

1. **Mustard seed faith.** Weymouth's Bible translation says in Luke 17:6,*"If you had faith that grows as a grain of mustard seed."* It is faith that grows as a mustard seed that can heal the sick, cast out demons and see signs following. *"And these signs shall follow them that believe; In my name shall they cast out devils; they shall speak with new tongues; They shall take up serpents; and if they drink any deadly thing, it shall not hurt them; they shall lay hands on the sick, and they shall recover"* [Mark 16:17 AKJV]. That's why, *"The kingdom of heaven is liked to a grain of mustard seed, which a man took, and sowed in his field: Which indeed is the least of all seeds: but when it is grown, it is the greatest among herbs, and becomes a tree, so that the birds of the air come and lodge in the branches thereof."* [Matt 13:31 AKJV]. The kingdom of God is a growing kingdom. So we don't need little faith but growing faith, so that we may move from "faith to faith" [Rom 1:17]. We move from faith to faith as our faith grows.

2. **Mountain Moving Faith.** *"Though I have all faith, so that I could remove mountains ..."* [1 Cor 13:2]. It took all, or total, or full grown faith to move mountains. That's why in Matthew 17:16-20 Jesus' disciples could not heal the boy. It was because of "unbelief" or little faith or undeveloped or immature faith. They needed more faith. Their faith needed growth.

3. **God Gives Seed Faith.** *"For I say through the grace given ... God hath death to every man a measure [seed] of faith"* [Rom 12:3]. A measure is a limited portion, that is, a seed of faith. No Christian can say, "I don't have faith." But this seed of faith that we have must grow. The most important question now is how do I make my faith grow?

There are two kinds of faith. The first is the gift of faith mentioned in 1 Cor 12:9. This is divine or sovereign impartation of a gift of faith from God to a person. We will look at this under the gifts of the Holy Spirit. The second is developed faith. This is the one that grows, and is available to every believer. Its growth is dependent on us.

- **Faith grows by obedience.** You will know the glory of God in your life only in proportion to the development of faith in your life. *"So the faith comes by hearing the word of God"* [Rom 10:17]. In this case hearing is not audio reception through the ear or through the mind when read or spoken, but it is to hear and act upon what has been heard. When faith comes it grows by obeying the word of God. This is demonstrated and expressed by hearing, and then acting upon what you have heard. Remember this is the God kind of faith. Disobedience hinders growth.

- **Faith grows by hearing.** *"Faith comes by hearing, and hearing by the word* (Rhema) *of God"* [Rom 10:"17]. For more detailed explanation read Romans chapter four. The Rhema word is the spoken word of God, the anointed message, or life giving word of God. Rhema is a Greek term that is often translated "word" in English versions of the New Testament. The more we hear, the more we know God, and the more we appreciate that God does not lie (he fulfils his word and his promises). Do not refuse his voice. Be ready for his voice. Tune in to his voice in prayer and by fasting. As a father he desires to speak to you.

- **Faith Grows by speaking.** *"And Jesus answering saith unto them, Have faith in God. For verily I say unto you, That whosoever shall say unto this mountain, Be thou removed, and be thou cast into the sea; and shall not doubt in his heart, but shall believe that those things which he saith shall come to pass; he shall have whatsoever he saith."* [Mark 11:22-23]. The faith of God is the faith that speaks. Speak what God says. Speak a word, then God will act on your word. That's how you overcome the devil by your word. Rev 12:11 says, *"They overcame him (the devil) by the blood of the* *lamb and by the word of their testimony."* We believe what we speak, and we speak what we believe. What we say is what we get because of our words. What we say determines the outcome of our situation. Jesus is the high priest of our confession [Heb 3:1]. He wants us to confess His Word. He makes intercession on behalf of us to the Father.

# 10.  WATER BAPTISM

## What is of Baptism?

Baptism *(baptismos*in Greek*)* means immersion or dipping an object in a liquid. This word was, and is used to refer to dipping cloth in dye in order to change its colour. Now water baptism is immersing [dipping, burying] a person in water after repentance from sin, and believing in Jesus. It is an outward sign [or expression] of:

❖ Identification with Jesus Christ in his death, burial and resurrection. *"Buried with him in baptism, wherein also ye are risen with him through the faith of the operation of God, who hath raised him from the dead"* [Col 2:12]. Romans 6:4 also says *"Therefore we are buried with him by baptism into death: that like as Christ was raised up from the dead by the glory of the Father, even so we also should walk in newness of life."* We die with Christ as we are being immersed. When we are under the water it means we are buried with Him and rising up from the water represents resurrection with him.

❖ Dying to sin, that is, it is your 'funeral service.' The old nature is buried in water and you arise in new life in Christ Jesus [2 Cor 5:17].

❖ Being clothed with Christ. For *"you are all sons of God through faith in Christ Jesus, for all of you were baptised into Christ have clothed yourselves with Christ"* [Gal 3:27].

❖ Inclusion into the united body of Christ. It is an outward sign of inward faith. By being baptised we join in the body of Christ. *"There is one body, and one Spirit, even as ye are called in one hope of your calling; One Lord, one faith, one baptism,"* [Eph 4:4-5].

❖ A symbol of inner cleansing and purification [Matt 28:19]. It means spiritual circumcision [Col 2:11-12]. Immersion in water also represents purity.

❖ Spiritual rebirth. *"He saved us through the washing of rebirth and renewal by the Holy Spirit."* Titus 3:5]. John 3:5 says that unless a man is born of water and spirit he cannot enter the Kingdom of God.

❖ Washing away of sins. *"And now what are you waiting for? Get up, be baptised and wash you sins away, calling on his name"* [Acts 22:16]. Water represents its general cleansing purpose, but in this case cleansing our sins.

## Some Old Testament symbols of Water Baptism

❑ **The Flood.** *"For Christ also hath once suffered for sins, the just for the unjust, that he might bring us to God, being put to death in the flesh, but quickened by the Spirit: By which also he went and preached unto the spirits in prison; Which sometime were disobedient, when once the longsuffering of God waited in the days of Noah, while the ark was a preparing, wherein few, that is, eight souls were saved by water. The like figure whereunto even baptism doth also now save us (not the putting away of the filth of the flesh, but the answer of a good conscience toward God,) by the resurrection of Jesus Christ"* [1 Peter 3:18-21]. Although the flood lifted the ark to safety, Noah and his family were saved by being in the ark. We are saved through being 'in Christ' not through the waters of baptism.

❑ **The Rite of Circumcision.** Every Israelite male child was supposed to be circumcised. It was the sign of the covenant with God. Now baptism is the new sign of circumcision. It is a sign to show that we are now children of God. The sign of baptism also acts as a sign of being the descendants of Abraham which we became after receiving Jesus Christ as our saviour [Col 2:11-12].

❑ **Crossing the Red Sea.** *"They were all baptised into Moses in the cloud and in the sea"* [1 Cor 10:2]. All the Israelites had to pass under the waters of the Red Sea for them to be delivered from the Egyptian army. When the Israelites entered the parted Red sea and walked through it, the Egyptians thought they had won, and could follow and finish them. But when the Israelites walked (rose) out of the Red sea as the sign of the resurrection of Jesus Christ, the waters closed in and swept away the Egyptians. This is a symbol of water baptism, as well as the power of the resurrection of Jesus Christ.

## Biblical Way of Baptism

The Greek word for baptism is *"baptizo"* which means to dip or to submerge, and not to pour or sprinkle. Neither does it mean waving a flag above a person. Waving a flag above a person is not baptism, and has nothing to do with baptism. There are other Greek words which mean to pour or sprinkle, but they do not mean the same as baptism. Only the act of immersion symbolises Christ's death, burial and resurrection, not the pouring or sprinkling of water. Romans 6:4 says, *"We are buried with Him by baptism unto death"* refers to immersion. When we bury someone we dig a six feet deep hole, and totally cover the body with soil. We do not sprinkle the body with some soil, and say we have buried someone. There has to be complete covering of the person with water.

In Matt 3:16 Jesus was baptised in the Jordan River at Bethbarah where there was lots of water. As soon as he was baptised, he came up out of the water. At that moment: 1) God opened the heavens for Him [that Jesus might have access to God for provision of all things necessary for the fulfilment of his earthly ministry], 2) God anointed Him with the Holy Spirit, symbolised by a dove which descended on Him [to empower Him for his earthly ministry], and 3) God acknowledged Jesus as his well beloved Son in whom He was well pleased [to give Him substantiation for his claims during his earthly ministry]. Jesus was baptised by immersion. The act of immersion is the only way of baptism that accurately portrays the truth symbolised by water baptism. All other so called methods do not really symbolise our identification with Christ's death, burial and resurrection.

## Reasons of Being Baptised
The main reason is that Jesus commanded baptism to be practised by his disciples until the end of the age [Matt 28:19-20]. The early church practised water baptism, so we should continue with the same practise. In Acts 2:41 three thousand were baptised, and in Acts 8:12, 38 Philip baptised the Ethiopian Eunuch. It is also to fulfil all righteousness [Matt 3:15, Acts 2:38].

Water baptism has spiritual significance, and facilitates the release of God's power. During water baptism believers are often delivered from oppressions, filled with the Holy Spirit and have a divine encounter with God.

## Is John's Baptism and the Christian Baptism the Same?
The answer is not really, they are different.
## John's Baptism:
1) Was the authority of the father [John 1:33]. The son was not yet revealed.
2) Was meant mostly for, or targeted the Jews.
3) Was to prepare Christ and his physical political kingdom [Matt 3:2-12].
4) Had a forward look.
5) Ended with John's imprisonment.
6) Was not acceptable after Pentecost [Acts 19:1-6].

**Christian baptism:**
1) Is by the authority of Christ [Matt 28:19].
2) Is for all believers [Matt 28:19].
3) Is to proclaim entrance into Christ and his spiritual kingdom [Col 2:13].
4) Has a backward look.
5) Is still being observed today.
6) Is acceptable after Pentecost [Acts 19:4-6].

## Who should be baptised?

➤ Only believers are to be baptised [Matt 28:19, Acts 2:41]. Baptising an unbeliever does not make the person a Christian. The person will be immersed a dry sinner and come out a wet sinner.

➤ Infants should not be baptised. There is no authority in the scripture for practising infant baptism. The Bible makes personal belief in Jesus Christ to be the prerequisite for baptism. Infants do not have the capacity to believe in Jesus, neither can they be accountable for their actions. Hence baptising infants will not make them Christians when they grow up.

➤ The whole household should not be baptised upon the belief in Christ of the head of the household. Household salvation in Acts 16:31-34 and 1 Cor 1:16, 16:15 indicates that all members of the household had to believe first.

Sometimes some Christians choose to be re-baptised. This is when either:
✓ You were baptised by an unbeliever,
✓ You were not yet saved when you were baptised, or
✓ You were not baptised by immersion in water.
✓ You did not really understand why.

## Who May Baptise

The authority to baptise was given to the church in Matt 28:19. Therefore every believer was commanded to, and can baptise. The orderly way for a local church to discharge its duties is through its leaders. In many circumstances any Christian may perform the act [Acts 8:38, 9:17-18].

The one baptising should say, *"I baptise you in the name of the Father, the Son and the Holy Spirit"* as commanded in Matt 28:19. The subject must be immersed once during baptism, not three times, since Christ died once and resurrected once. If you were not properly baptised you might feel that you want a proper baptism.

# 11. THE HOLY SPIRIT

## Introduction

From the book of Genesis to Revelation the Bible talks about the Holy Spirit, yet little is known and few sermons are preached on the Holy Spirit. When you mention the Holy Spirit many people, even church leaders close their ears to you. Is the Holy Spirit a force or energy? Through the next two chapters we will look closely on this topic. Open your heart and mind as we go through the Bible exploring the Holy Spirit.

Who is the Holy Spirit [He]? The Holy Spirit is the Spirit of God *[bagios pneumatos*in Greek]. He is a person and has a personality. He has intellect, emotions and will. Therefore, he is not just a power or an influence. Even Jesus said it in John 14:26 Amp, *"But the Comforter (Counselor, Helper, Intercessor, Advocate, Strengthener, Standby), the Holy Spirit, Whom the Father will send in My name [in My place, to represent Me and act on My behalf], He will teach you all things. And He will cause you to recall (will remind you of, bring to your remembrance) everything I have told you."* He is indeed a person.

❑ **He is God.** He is called God in Acts 5:3-4 and 1 Cor 3:16. In Psalms 139:1-18 God and the Holy Spirit are intermixed. And is shown as having the characteristics of God, eternal, omnipresent [is everywhere], omnipotent [all powerful] and omniscient [knows everything]. 1 Corinthians 2:9-11 tells us that the Spirit reveals the deep things of God and knows all about God. He is equal to the Father and the son [Matt 28:19-20, 1 Cor 12:4-6, Rev 1:4-5].

❑ **He does the work of God.** He creates [Gen 1:2, Job 33:4] and gives life [Eze 37:1-11, John 20:22]. He causes rebirth [John 3:5-8]. He resurrects [Rom 8:11].

❑ **He is a person.** He has a mind and can pray with intercession [Rom 8:26-27]. He has a will [1 Cor 12:11] and feelings which can be hurt [Eph 4:30]. He can speak [Rev 2:7], teach [John 16:13], comfort [John 14:16], commands [Acts 16:6-7], be lied to [Acts 5:3] and be blasphemed or spoken about badly [Matt 12:31-32].

❑ **He has titles.** According to the above duties he is the :
   - Comforter who give strength i.e.*parakletos* [helper] – John 14:16.
   - Spirit of grace – Heb 10:29, Zech 12:10.
   - Spirit of life and Spirit of adoption – Rom 8:2, 15.

- Spirit of truth – John 14:17.
- Spirit of glory – 1 Peter 4:14
- Spirit of God – Gen 1:2.
- Spirit of your Father – Matt 10:20.
- Spirit of holiness – Rom 1:4.
- ❏ **He has symbols.** Normally are from His personality:
  - **Fire;** purging, purify, boldness, zealous, awesome – Matt 3:11, Acts 2:3.
  - **Wind;** unseen except for its results, regenerating, powerful – Acts 2:2.
  - **Water;** cleansing, refreshing, quenching of thirst, making fruitfulness possible – John 4:14, 7:38-39.
  - **A seal**; ownership, security – Eph 1:13, 4:30, 2 Tim 2:19.
  - **Oil;** usefulness, fruitfulness, beauty aid, food, fuel for light, healing – Psalms 104:15, Matt 25:1-13.
  - **A dove;** gentleness, tenderness, loveliness, mildness, peace – Matt 3:16, Mark 1:10, Luke 3:22, John 1:32.

You can relate to him. God desires us to fellowship with Him through the Holy Spirit [2 Cor 13:14]. He is waiting for you to jump in and drink till you cup overflows with the waters of life. *"In the last day, that great day of the feast, Jesus stood and cried, saying, if any man thirst, let him come unto me, and drink. He that believeth on me, as the scripture hath said, out of his belly shall flow rivers of living water. (But this spake he of the Spirit, which they that believe on Him should receive: for the Holy Ghost was not yet given; because that Jesus was not yet glorified.)"* [John 7:37-39]. Jesus meant the Holy Spirit, a free gift which everyone is invited to drink.

### The Holy Spirit in the Old Testament
The Holy Spirit is the same in the Old and New Testament. In the Old Testament we see in part the activities of the Holy Spirit. He empowered certain selected individuals for a limited time and for very special purposes. He strove with the sinners of Noah's days for 120 years [Gen 6:3]. He gave understanding to, and inspired men [Job 32:8]. Men of God were stirred, anointed indwelled and filled as he came upon them. The Holy Spirit power transformed them.

These are some of the Spirit empowered people:
- ❖ Joseph: Given discretion and wisdom by the Spirit – Gen 41:38-40.
- ❖ Bezalel: Given wisdom, understanding, knowledge and ability for beautiful workmanship by the Spirit- Ex 35:30-31.

- ❖ Moses: Anointed with the Holy Spirit. God then transferred the Spirit that was in Moses to seventy other men – Num 11:16-17.
- ❖ Joshua: had the Spirit within him. He was given special commission to lead God's people – Num 27:18-22, Deut 34:9.
- ❖ Othniel: Enabled by the Spirit to be a judge over Israel and to have victory in battle – Judges 3:9-10.
- ❖ Gideon: A simple, humble man who was anointed by the Spirit to be a great, victorious leader –Judges 6:15-16,34.
- ❖ Jepthan: Given boldness by the Spirit – Judges 11:29, 32.
- ❖ Samson: Given tremendous strength by the Holy Spirit, his uncut hair was a symbol of his Nazareth vows of obedience to God – Judges 13:24-25, 14:6, 19, 15:14.
- ❖ Saul: Had a complete personality change and prophesied, because of the Spirit coming upon him – 1 Sam 10:6.
- ❖ Elijah and Elisha: Did miracles through the power of the Holy Spirit. When Elijah was departing [2 King 2:9-15], Elisha asked for a double portion, but had been anointed already [2 Kings 19:16]. The result is that Elijah had eight miracles and Elisha ten miracles recorded [even after his death].

## The Holy Spirit in Jesus Christ

The Old Testament is a shadow pointing to Jesus, the anointed one. On Him the Holy Spirit cannot be quantitatively measured because God gave Him the Spirit without limit [John 3:34]. Jesus is a member of the trinity therefore he is also the Holy Spirit. His virgin birth was not natural, but by the power of the Holy spirit. When Jesus was being baptised, the Holy Spirit descended upon Him as a dove, and God put a seal on him. The Spirit then led Him into the wilderness. There he overcame temptation by the Holy Spirit's power. The Holy Spirit was not yet poured out, so Jesus was the first person to become infilled with the Holy Spirit.

Why did Jesus need to be filled by the Holy Spirit? Jesus came as a human [Phil 2:6-7]. He had to depend on the Holy Spirit as we should do. The anointing prophesied in Isaiah 42:1 was fulfilled at his baptism. This is his source of power. His resurrection was also achieved by the Holy Spirit [Rom 8:18].

## The Power of the Holy Spirit

The only way to receive God's blessing is by trusting in him. One thing God will never do is to lie. He fulfils his word. Joel 2:28-29 says, *"And it shall come to pass afterward, that I will pour out my spirit upon all flesh; and your sons and your daughters shall prophesy, your old men shall dream dreams, your young men shall see visions: And also upon the servants and upon the handmaids in those days will I pour out my spirit."* The Spirit of God was to be poured upon all [not certain] people. *"Thus saith the Lord that made thee, and formed thee from the womb, which will help thee; Fear not, O Jacob, my servant; and thou, Jesurun, whom I have chosen. For I will pour water upon him that is thirsty, and floods upon the dry ground: I will pour my spirit upon thy seed, and my blessing upon thine offspring"* [Isa 44:2-3]. Therefore you can be baptised with the Holy Spirit.

Who baptised in the Holy Spirit? It is Jesus [Matt 3:11]. He is the one who was to come and baptised with the Holy Spirit and fire. We can't earn Him by good deeds but by trusting God. The Holy Spirit is the promised helper or comforter in John 14. He will be in you [John 14:17] and he also reveals to us things from Jesus. Do you want to know Jesus? If you say 'yes' then you need to be baptised with the Holy Spirit. He is important to you. Jesus' final command carried this promise for you [Luke 24:49, Acts 1:4-9]. Can all people receive the Holy Spirit? Yes, as long as you ask, [Luke 11:13] obey [Acts 5:31-32], and believe [Gal 3:13-14].

## The Meaning of Pentecost

In Acts 2:1-4 the promise of the Holy Spirit was fulfilled. *"And when the day of Pentecost was fully come, they were all with one accord in one place. And suddenly there came a sound from heaven as of a rushing mighty wind, and it filled all the house where they were sitting. And there appeared unto them cloven tongues like as of fire, and it sat upon each of them. And they were all filled with the Holy Ghost, and began to speak with other tongues, as the Spirit gave them utterance"* [Acts 2:1-4]. This is the day the church was born.

Why did God choose that day for the birth of the church? Pentecost means the 50th day in Latin that is after Jewish Passover [or feast weeks]. In the Bible seven means completeness and the 50th day is the first day after 7 x 7 =49 days. During the feast of Passover [Exodus 12:1-14] the blood of the lamb represents the blood of Jesus. On Pentecost day about 1300 years before, Moses had been given law at Mount Sinai [the Old Testament church was formed]. The law is a shadow of things to come. Pentecost was a divine appointment for those who came for the feast from every nation [Acts 2:5]. When Peter preached after being transformed by the Holy Spirit 3000 people of different nationalities were saved. Therefore the day of Pentecost had been strategically appointed by God for a divine purpose.

## The Baptism of the Holy Spirit

We must take a step of faith to move into the baptism of the Holy Spirit. The baptism of the Holy Spirit is like stepping into another room, or opening eyes which had been closed. It can only occur after, or during repentance. To baptise [from baptiso in Greek] means to dip or immerse as in dyeing. When you deep something in a liquid, it takes the colour of the liquid, in this case you become like Jesus. Immersion in water, removes dryness implies that spiritual dryness is removed. The baptism of the Holy Spirit is actually the baptism in the Holy Spirit. If the baptism of the Holy Spirit is good enough for servants of God in the book of Acts then it's good enough for you and me as well.

Other terms of the Holy Spirit baptism:
- Endued [clothed] with power from on high [Luke 24:49],
- Receive power [Acts 1:8],
- Filled with the Holy Spirit [Acts 2:4],
- Receive the gift of the Holy Spirit [Acts 2:38-39],
- He was fallen upon [Acts 8:16],
- Was poured out [Acts 10:45].

There are two parts to a gift, giving and receiving. God gives and as we receive the Holy Spirit we have an encounter with Jesus. The Holy Spirit was given to the church on the day of Pentecost. One can be baptised with the Holy Spirit before being baptised in water as in Acts 10:44-48. Let's compare water baptism and Holy Spirit baptism.

During water baptism the believer is baptised by a man (or minister), as a witness to conversion and remission of sin. It indicates entry into the body of Christ. However, during the Holy Spirit baptism the believer (usually already baptised in water) is baptised by Jesus himself, to cloth him with power. It results in the receiving of the power and the gifts of the Holy Spirit.

We see that the baptism in the Holy Spirit is actually an encounter with Jesus. He is the baptiser in the Holy Spirit and not a man. Every believer has the Holy Spirit [1 Cor 12:13, Rom 8:9] but not every believer is baptised with the

Holy Spirit. John 14:17 says that he will be in [not with] the believer after baptism in the Holy Spirit. The disciples' relations with the Holy Spirit changed from having the spirit dwelling with them, to in them. The examples below show the difference between an ordinary believer and a Holy Spirit baptised believer:

❖ Well of water [John 4:14, Isa 12:3]   = salvation
❖ Rivers of water [John 7:38-39] = Holy Spirit.

Which of these two sources has more water? It is the river.

The Holy Spirit is imparted by prayerfully waiting in one accord [Acts 1:12-14, 2:1-4], the laying on of hands [Acts 8:17] or powerful anointed preaching [Acts 10]. In general there are many ways, even when praying alone, kneeling, out in the mountains or in the forest. There is no need to worry about laying on of hands. From Isaiah 44:3 what is necessary is to have a desire [John 7:37-38]. The Old Testament evidence of baptism was prophesying [1 Sam 10:10]. The New Testament evidence is speaking in other tongues [Acts 2:1-11], miracles [Acts 8:14-19], knowing it by the spirit [Acts 2:39]. Are you willing to die for Christ? In Acts 1:8 a witness is a martyr [giving up life] for Christ. The Holy Spirit moves you from the natural to the supernatural realm. He brings scripture to life as you study the word of God. He imparts new spiritual sensitivity, gives more power and effectiveness in prayer. He makes you aware of Satan's activities and how to resist him. He glorifies Jesus and reveals more of his personality. He brings more joy, assurance, peace, faith and desire to seek God. Above all this, he gives power to witness.

### How to be baptised with the Holy Spirit
Let me ask you a question. Do you live in a wicked and rebellious generation today? If you answer is 'yes,' there is a great need for the Holy Spirit to enable you to live in this world. The promise of the spirit is for those far off, in terms of distance, race, in time or from God [Acts 2:38-40]. You are one of these. The promise is for you. This is not an experiment. Do you desire the Holy Spirit in his fullness and believe you can have him? Be honest with yourself. If you do not have the desire, or you do not believe then it is not going to work.

God really wants to empower you. Are you ready? Follow the steps below one by one:

- **Seek God** – [Isaiah 55:6] Take a step towards God and he will come to you. Read Phil 3:13 as you initiate a search for God. Jeremiah 29:13-14 say, *"And ye shall seek me, and find me, when ye shall search for me with all your heart. And I will be found of you, saith the Lord."* Do not seek blessing, but Him.
- **Repent** – Turn away from past sins. Be genuinely sorry for the sins you committed. Denounce the works of darkness, false religions, witchcraft, occult etc
- **Be baptised in water** – [Acts 2:28] It is an outward sign of being born again. Be baptised in his death, buried with Christ and rise with him in newness of life.
- **Be baptised in the Holy Spirit** – [Luke 11:9-10] this is the way forward. I believe you are hungry for the baptism in the Holy Spirit by now. This is not an emotional experience, it is the Spirit of Jesus Christ that you receive. The result of the baptism is the increased ability to be a true witness to Christ's love and power, as well as living a victorious personal life. This step is very important especially for leaders.
- **Grow in the fruit and gifts of the Holy Spirit** – [Romans 8:26-27] After Holy Spirit baptism, the fruit and gift should be an everyday part of your walk and ministry, respectively. Pray in the Spirit, it can be your own language, or with groans, or silent prayer, or singing a prayer [Eph 6:18-19]. Psalms are in the Bible, church hymns, spiritual songs are words and melodies given by the Holy Spirit in known language. They are for praise and worship. Pray also in tongues.
- **Spread the gospel of Jesus Christ** – Matt 28:19-20 is the great commission. The last command from Jesus is *"every creature to preach to every creature"* [Mark 16:15].

Make sure you move in the above seven steps. If you are on one step, move then to the next. Do not stop, or else you fall. Take a step of faith and penetrate that ceiling, and limitations in faith. Some steps like repentance need continuous re-visitations, whilst one step like water baptism and Holy Spirit baptism might come before another. Press in towards Jesus and know Him personally. Remember spiritual things can only be understood by a spiritual mind. The Holy Spirit prepares you for spiritual warfare.

It's a fact that:
- He is your mentor [John 14:26].
- He is a gift from the father, to a child (the believer) [Acts 2:38, 10:45].
- He only enters by a personal invitation [Luke 11:13].
- He is not a dove, a vapour or cloud, but a person who thinks, teaches and talks [John 16:13].
- He inspired men to write the scriptures [Acts 1:16, 2 Tim 3:16].
- His presence produces joy [Psalms 16:11, Gal 5:22].

## Are Tongues for Everyone?

There is no direct answer in the Bible, and it is not mentioned either. Many people today base tongues as the sole evidence of the baptism of the Holy Spirit from Acts 2:4, 10:46, 19:6. But in many instances also do not mention anything about speaking in tongues [Acts 4:23, 8:14-39, 9:1-42, 17, 32]. Therefore speaking in tongues is not a solid, perfect, confirmation but it is a general accepted confirmation since most people who are baptised with the Holy Spirit instantly start to speak in tongues. However in many cases one can be baptised after the laying on of hands, and not speaks immediately. This means that they have the gift of speaking in tongues, but cannot exercise it. Everyone who is baptised has the capacity and potential to speak in tongues.

Desire not just to speak in tongues but to operate in the other gifts of the Holy Spirit as well. This is what we will look at in the next chapter.

## 12. THE POWER OF THE HOLY SPIRIT

There is great power in the anointing of the Holy Spirit, great power that no man has ever fully experienced. This is the power that has transformed many people over the years. Once the Holy Spirit comes upon you, you will never be the same again. In this section we look at this secret power, and how we can tap it to benefit humanity.

### The Fruit of the Holy Spirit

After the baptism in the Holy Spirit, what next? How best can we use such great power? From Galatians 22-23 Amp says, *"But the fruit of the [Holy] Spirit [the work which His presence within accomplishes] is love, joy (gladness), peace, patience (an even temper, forbearance), kindness, goodness (benevolence), faithfulness, gentleness (meekness, humility), self-control (self-restraint, continence). Against such things there is no law [that can bring a charge]."* The fruit comes from and because of the presence of the Holy Spirit dwelling inside a Christian believer and yielding to him. It is not by our own effort.

The fruit has nine parts listed below:
1. Love – Brotherly love or human affection, sacrificing kind of love, divine love [Christian love] – 1 Cor 13, John 15:13.
2. Joy – Inner joy independent of circumstance. It is the joy of the Lord – John 15:11, Neh 8:10.
3. Peace – Inside peace even in turmoil situations – John 14:27, Phil 4:7, Romans 5:1.
4. Long suffering [patience] – Heb 6:12, Psalms 27:14.
5. Gentleness [kindness] – Isaiah 40:11, Psalms 18:35.
6. Goodness – Luke 18:18-19, Eph 5:8-11.
7. Faith [faithfulness] – Prov 11:13, 1 Cor 4:1-2, Heb 11.
8. Meekness [humility] – Matt 11:29, Titus 3:2, 2 Tim 2:24-25.
9. Temperance [self-control] – Acts 24:25.

The Holy Spirit also enables you to have these three characteristics as well:
- ❖ Righteousness and holiness – Romans 14:17, 1 John 1:5.
- ❖ Contentment and thankfulness – this includes praise – 1 Tim 6:6, Psalms 100:4-5.
- ❖ Power [authority] – 1 Cor 4:20, 2 Tim 1:7, Acts 1:8.

## The Gifts of the Holy Spirit

*"Thou hast ascended on high, thou hast led captivity captive: thou hast received gifts for men; yea, for the rebellious also, that the Lord God might dwell among them"* [Psalms 68:18]. Christ ascended so that he may set the captives free, send gifts of the Holy Spirit, and God may dwell in us through the Holy Spirit. This perfects the church for service. Nobody owns or possesses a spiritual gift, but we are simply conduits or vessels which carry them as stated in 2 Corinthians 4:7. We do not have just one gift, but many. The best gift is the one that fills a particular need at a particular time. This is the gift that we should desire [1 Cor 12:31].

1 Corinthians 12:4-6 says that, *"Now there are diversities of gifts, but the same Spirit. And there are differences of administrations, but the same Lord. And there are diversities of operations, but it is the same God which worketh all in all."* From these scriptures we see that there are three kinds of spiritual gifts:
1. According to diversities [kinds] of gifts, but the same Spirit – 1 Cor 12:7-10.
2. Differences of administrations [services], but the same Lord [Jesus] – Eph 4:7-11.
3. Diversities of operations [workings], but it is the same God [the father] – Rom 12:6-8. These are also called motivation gifts.

### 1. Diversities of the Gifts from the Holy Sprit

These are supernatural gifts which do not depend on back ground or ancestors of a person but are given by the Holy Spirit. Spiritual gifts are not bound by natural rules and are unpredictable.

### Revelation Gifts
❖ Word of Wisdom; is a supernatural revelation of the mind for the purpose and will of God. God's solution to a problem is revealed. It spells out practical actions required to solve the problem.
❖ Word of Knowledge; is a supernatural revelation of the existence, or nature of a person or situation. It involves spiritual insights, information and knowledge of something, with no way of knowing through experience or natural observation.
❖ Discerning of spirits; enables one to know what spirit is empowering, or motivating, or operating in a person or behind a manifestation or activity. There is an ability to see into the realm of the spirit.

## Power Gifts
❖ Gift of faith. This is an extra ordinary faith. It is a supernatural unwavering faith or trust in God that results in miracles. This gift enables one to trust God for great things, to cast out devils, or speak words that come to pass.
❖ Gift of working of miracles. This gift enables one to alter, override and suspend laws of nature. Occurrences that never occur by natural means happen. This is the Holy Spirit's holding and works.
❖ Gift of healing. People are totally healed often instantly. This is not only physical but also spiritual healing.

## Utterance Gifts
❖ Diverse kinds of tongues. The anointing makes you speak in many different tongues. Tongues are unlearnt languages given by the Holy Spirit alone, and cannot be understood directly by the speaker. They are for prayer to God, singing to God, blessing the Lord or giving thanks to God. They can be interpreted.
❖ Interpretation of tongues. This is not a direct translation but general meaning of words spoken in tongues. Tongues that are interpreted become prophecy. You may interpret your own tongue or another person's tongues.
❖ Gift of Prophecy. This involves speaking words that God gives you. Prophecy must agree with the Scriptures. It builds up, stirs up, or cheers us up, by speaking about future things and reveals the present as well.

## 2. Difference of Administration from the Son
These are listed in Ephesians 4:7, 11-12,*"But unto every one of us is given grace according to the measure of the gift of Christ. ... And he gave some, apostles; and some, prophets; and some, evangelists; and some, pastors and teachers; For the perfecting of the saints, for the work of the ministry, for the edifying of the body of Christ."* They are often called administration gifts or offices.

## 3. Diversities of Operations from the Father
These are in Romans 12:4-8. *"For as we have many members in one body, and all members have not the same office: So we, being many, are one body in Christ, and every one members one of another. Having then gifts differing according to the grace that is given to us, whether prophecy, let us prophesy according to the proportion of faith; Or ministry, let us wait on our ministering: or he that teaches, on teaching; Or he that exhorteth, on exhortation: he that gives, let him do it with simplicity; he that ruleth, with diligence; he that*

*showeth mercy, with cheerfulness."* They are often called services gifts. They include natural talents and can be developed as one grows up, learnt or shaped by the environment that surrounds a person.

## The Power of the Holy Spirit
The Holy Spirit [God in action] is action orientated, and Jesus was a dynamic, Satan conquering Lord. He was not a sloppy conforming person. Demons tremble before Him because of the power of the Holy Spirit operating in him. This is the calling card for the kingdom of God. The expansion of the kingdom of God [defeat of Satan] depends on the number of Christians moving in the power of the Holy Spirit. The apostles had more than three years of institutional training, instruction, theory and practice that Jesus complemented with his final intensive 40 days seminar before he ascended into heaven, but Jesus told them to wait for the power of the Holy Spirit.

Power increases as we exercise what God has given us. This is good stewardship. Jesus' ministry was and is of two parts; 1) Declaration: - preaching repentance, and the Good News of the kingdom. 2) Demonstration: - [of the power of the Holy Spirit] casting devils, healing etc.

Some examples of the demonstration of the power of the Holy Spirit in the book of Acts and the results:
**Signs and wonders;**
- By disciples [Acts 2:43] resulted in daily adding to church [Acts 2:47].
- Power of God shown in mighty works [Acts 4:33], resulted in the church in Samaria [Acts 8:12].
- Hand of the Lord with them [Acts 11:20, 13:11], resulted in great number that believed and turned to the Lord [Acts 11:21].
- By Paul and Barnabas [Acts 14:1-7], resulted in believers [Acts 14:4].

**Speaking Gifts;**
- Tongues [Acts 10:44], resulted in baptised believers [Acts 10:47].
- Prophecy [Acts 13:1], resulted in conversion of John's disciples [Acts 19:5-7].
- Pentecost [Acts 2], resulted in many being baptised [Acts 2:4, 4:1].

**Healing;**
- Lame man walk [Acts 3:7-9], resulted in 5000 believers added [Acts 4:4].
- Sick and unclean spirit [Acts 5:16], resulted in healing of many [Acts 5:16].
- Demon expelled [Acts 16:18], encouragement of brethren [Acts 16:40].

**Miracles;**
- Ananias and Sapphire [Acts 5:1-11], resulted in fear of God [Acts 5:13].
- Elymas blinded [Acts 13:4-12], resulted in Sergius Paulus believing.
- Paul stoned and raised [Acts 14:19-20], resulted in more disciples [Acts 14:21].
- Viper bit Paul [Acts 28], resulted in church in Malta Island [Acts 28:3-10].

**Dead raised;**
- Dorcas raised [Acts 9] resulted in many believing [Acts 9:40-42].

From these examples we see that the power of the Holy Spirit results in dramatic church growth. It is the catalyst for effective evangelism, and this is what we need in this day. This is the missing ingredient in today's church. If you have a taste of the power of the Holy Spirit, you will never accept anything less.

<u>**Manifestation of the Power of the Holy Spirit**</u>
Just as wind, though not seen, its effects are seen, so is the Holy Spirit. Signs and wonders accompany the presence of the Holy Spirit. Some of them are below:
1. **Shaking and trembling:** This may be accompanied by tears and speaking in tongues. [Psalms 2:11, Jer 5:22, 23:9, Dan 10:10-11, Mark 5:33, Luke 8:47, Acts 9:6, 16:29, 1 Cor 2:3].
2. **Speechlessness** [2 Chr 5:13-14].
3. **Drunkenness:** This is accompanied by laughing and crying. [Jer 23:9, Luke 5:37, Acts 2:13, Eph 5:18].
4. **Groaning:** The Spirit of intercession causes one to groan in travail. This will cause the "birth process." Jesus also groaned at Lazarus tomb. [Jer 30:6, Psalms 55:2, Isa 42:14, John 11:33-38, Rom 8:22-27, 2 Cor 5:2-5, Gal 4:19, Heb 5:7].
5. **Falling;** is the most common. This happens to all classes of people or ages. The presence of God results in weakness or falling. [Gen 17:17, Dan 11:7-16, Luke 5:8, 8:47, John 18:6, Acts 9:4].
6. **Holy laughter:** This is a loud hearty laughter, with tears. [Gen 17:17, 21:6, Job 5:22, 1 the 5:16, Acts 13:52 Rev 1:17].
7. **Singing:** This is unaccountable and the person is in joyous state. [Job 5:22, Psalms 2:4, 37:13, 63:3, Heb 12:2, 1 Peter 1:8].

We do not have to put more focus on these manifestations, but it is the transformed life and service that is important. The devil can imitate these manifestations as well, therefore discern the spirit [1 Th 5:20-22].

## What to Be Aware Of

The Holy Spirit is a powerful and sensitive person. Do not quench him. How then can we live with Him without quenching him? It is Him who knows the answer. Ask him. *"Wherefore I say unto you, all manner of sin and blasphemy shall be forgiven unto men: but the blasphemy against the Holy Ghost shall not be forgiven unto men. And whosoever speaketh a word against the Son of man, it shall be forgiven him: but whosoever speaketh against the Holy Ghost, it shall not be forgiven him, neither in this world, neither in the world to come"* [Matt 12:31-32]. *"And grieve not the Holy Spirit of God, whereby ye are sealed unto the day of redemption"* [Eph 4:30]. *"Quench not the Spirit. Despise not prophesying. Prove all things; hold fast that which is good"* [1Thess 5:19-21].

Build yourself on the rock of God's revelation, the Word of God. *"Therefore whosoever heareth these sayings of mine, and doeth them, I will liken him unto a wise man, which built his house upon a rock: And the rain descended, and the floods came, and the winds blew, and beat upon that house; and it fell not: for it was founded upon a rock. And every one that heareth these sayings of mine, and doeth them not, shall be likened unto a foolish man, which built his house upon the sand: And the rain descended, and the floods came, and the winds blew, and beat upon that house; and it fell: and great was the fall of it"* [Matt 7:24-27]. Do not focus on experiences. What if they are not there? We do not build on the Holy Spirit but he helps us to build on the Word of God.

Remember; zealots are not wise. They cause others to stumble. Beware of some manifestations that are not of God, but from demons. Prophecy must be judged in line with the word of God. Direction must be from God as one is led by the Holy Spirit. Carnal power and glory hunger can cause divisions in church. Commandments must be obeyed because the Holy Spirit does not contradict the scriptures. Some gifts are not being used effectively. All gifts are very important and relevant. Be a witness for Jesus Christ so as to fulfil the great commission.

### Lastly
The Holy Spirit is preparing for the coming of the king [Jesus]. John prepared the way for the physical coming of the Lord Jesus, that is, his kingdom on earth. But today it's the Holy Spirit, God himself who is making a spiritual way for the coming of Jesus Christ, preparing the church for the kingdom of heaven. Just as those who rejected John's baptism and repentance, some are refusing the Holy Spirit baptism today. They were refusing in John's time. They are doing the same in this day.

The Holy Spirit is holding back the manifestation of the spirit of iniquity [lawlessness], and keeping this spirit from taking [culminating] in *the man of sin [lawlessness].* When the church is taken away [at rapture], the restrainer, the Holy Spirit, will also be taken away [back to heaven] and "the man of sin" will come on the scene with no restrain [2 Thess 2:7].

## 13.  PRAYER, FASTING AND SPIRITUAL WARFARE

### What is Prayer

Prayer is communication with God, which includes listening to his word, worshipping, adoring and petitioning him, as well as confessing sins, and interceding for others. It can simply be defined as fellowship with God. In the Old Testament it is referred to as *"calling upon the name of the Lord"* [Gen 15:2, 18:23], to intercede for Israel [Exodus 32:11-12], or to seek the face of the Lord [Psalms 100:2, 63:1].

Prayer is regarded in the New Testament as absolutely essential for all believers, and they are commanded to pray continually [1 Thess 5:17]. Personal or individual fellowship with God is needed. Prayerlessness can lead to the worshipping of idols. Prayer changes those who pray. The time we spent with God in prayer can release the most dynamic, history changing power this world has ever known. Prayer has the power to determine, change and affect your destiny and your future. This is the weapon that makes the devil tremble. This is the weapon that can confuse our foe. This is the way to dissolve our problems and situations. The power to victory is in our mouth. All men of power are men of prayer. This is the power in prayer.

Why should we pray? The most important reason is that we are commanded by God to pray and it is essential for all believers [Matt 6:5]. It opens the channels of God's power. Absence of prayer means absence of God's power [Acts 4:23-31]. Prayer is evidence of true commitment, that is, the 'I don't depend on my own but on God' attitude. It creates fellowship with God. It makes us know God and brings us closer to him. We become co-labourers with God as we work in hand with him [1 Cor 3:9]. Prayer renews us spiritually. Burdens are removed, and you fill free afterwards. It is true that the deeper the prayer life, the taller the spiritual life.

### Conditions for Effective Prayer
- **Holiness** – means separate from sin, and set apart for a special purpose. Separation and purity is the core of holiness. [Psalms 24:3-4, Isa 59:2, John 9:30-31]. Holiness is essential for prayer to be effective. God can neither listen nor look at a sinner.
- **Persistence and boldness** – Luke 11:5-8 shows that continuing in a habit or course of action in spite of opposition. Eph 6:18 says "keep on praying."

- **Fervency** – is showing intense or strong feeling, that is, from the bottom of the heart. *"The effectual fervent prayer of a righteous man availeth much"* [James 5:16].
- **Right motive** – Pray not out of selfish motives. *"And when thou prayest, thou shalt not be as the hypocrites are: for they love to pray standing in the synagogues and in the corners of the streets, that they may be seen of men. Verily I say unto you, they have their reward. But thou, when thou prayest, enter into thy closet, and when thou hast shut thy door, pray to thy Father which is in secret; and thy Father which seeth in secret shall reward thee openly. But when ye pray, use not vain repetitions, as the heathen do: for they think that they shall be heard for their much speaking. Be not ye therefore like unto them: for your Father knoweth what things ye have need of, before ye ask him"* [Matt 6:5-8]. James 4:3 says, *"Ye ask, and receive not, because ye ask amiss, that ye may consume it upon your lusts."*
- **Faith** – is trust in God. *"But let him ask in faith, nothing wavering. For he that wavereth is like a wave of the sea driven with the wind and tossed. For let not that man think that he shall receive any thing of the Lord. A double minded man is unstable in all his ways"* [James 1:6-8].

## When Do We Pray?

Many heroes of faith in the Bible, can be observed to have had regular times of the day set aside specifically for prayer. Often these are the three set periods a day, in the morning, noon and evening. *"As for me, I will call upon God; and the Lord shall save me. Evening, and morning, and at noon, will I pray, and cry aloud: and he shall hear my voice"* [Psalms 55:16]. Pray at all times. Jesus kept the heaven open for anointing through the rest of his life by prayer [Luke 3:21-22]. We need to *"keep on praying in the spirit"* [Eph 6:18]. Examples of Jesus praying:
⇨ Early in the morning [Mark 1:35].
⇨ Before each meal [Mark 6:42
⇨ All night [Luke 6:12].
⇨ Before choosing his disciples [Luke 6:12-13].
⇨ Before crucifixion [Luke 22:39-44].
⇨ Before the beginning [in the wilderness] and he end of his ministry [in the garden of Gethsemane].

There is no special prayer posture. Like fasting, prayer is a time of humility before God, and generally the prayer position shows our dependence on God.
⇨ On the face [Num 20:6, Deut 9:25, Matt 26:39].
⇨ Face between knees [1 Kings 18:42].

⇨ Bowing down [Gen 24:26, Exodus 4:31, 12:27].
⇨ Kneeling [1 Kings 8:54, Isa 45:23, Luke 22:41, Eph 3:14].
⇨ Standing [1 Kings 8:22, Mark 11:25, Luke 18:11].
⇨ Lifted hands [Psalms 28:2, Lam 2:19, 1 Tim 2:8].

The inner attitude is more important than the outer posture. The required approach is of humility [not for show], in faith with truth and confidence. We ought to have forgiven [Matt 6:12] and proper heart [Jer 29:13, Heb 10:2].

## What is Fasting?
Fasting is the abstinence from food for religious purposes. It generally means denying our bodies some of its usual provision. To go without food for religious reasons usually shows humility, penitence or grief. Fasting is accompanied by prayer; otherwise it is just a 'hunger strike.' Fasting sharpens our receptivity to God's word and spiritual signals. Faith unlocks the faith in you. When our motive is to draw closer to God, we will hear more clearly the voice of the Lord.

Paul in 1 Thess 5:23, refers to man as spirit [the inward part of man that is God conscious], soul [intellect, will and emotions, the inward part of man that is self-conscious] and body [responding through the senses that part of us that make us world conscious]. Fasting reduces the activities of the body and re-orientates the soul, thereby drawing us near to the spiritual world where we can then communicate and fellowship with God. In this state we are more effective, warring with spiritual forces by using spiritual laws, and override the laws of nature. The Bible mentions four types of fast (1) denying oneself food and water [Exodus 34:28, Deut 9:9], (2) denying oneself food [Matt 4:1-2], (3) denying certain pleasant foods [Dan 10:3] and (4) married people may fast from sex for a time by mutual consent in order to pray [1 Cor 7:4-5].

## True Fasting [Isaiah 58:3-12]
Wrong fasting is unacceptable to God because it humbles the outward man, but does not humble the inner man to obey and love other people. Fasting unaccompanied by true worship and just treatment of fellow man, is also unnoticed by God. This is what the Israelites were doing. They started to ask God why their prayers were not being answered.

True fasting is accompanied by separating ourselves from all that is evil and dedicating ourselves to all that is good. It humbles the body. We are to do the Lord's pleasure, not our own. Evil works are not permitted during fasting. This

is the kind of fasting that is acceptable to God. These are the characteristics of a proper fast:
- ❖ It is done in secret, and will be rewarded openly.
- ❖ Stop oppressing workers, and doing unjust deeds.
- ❖ Helping others in practical way.
- ❖ Involves personal sanctification.

The benefits [from God] of a proper fast are; good health, protection in front and behind, guidance and spiritual drink, in times of spiritual drought. Some of the examples of fast in the Bible are listed below:
- ⇨ Daniel – to gain understanding of a vision [Dan 10:3].
- ⇨ Ezra – mourning over unfaithfulness of Israel [Ezra 10:6].
- ⇨ Ester – before appearing before the king [Ester 4:16].
- ⇨ Paul – after he met the Lord, fasted for three days while blind [Acts 9:9].
- ⇨ Leaders of the Antioch church – sending out Barnabas and Paul [Acts 13:23].
- ⇨ Paul and Barnabas – appointing elders [Acts 14:23].

## Extraordinary Fasts
The three forty day fasting mentioned in the Bible were all of a miraculous nature and initiated by God. God through the Holy Spirit moved these men to fast. It was through divine appointment:
- ⇨ Moses while receiving the Ten Commandments [Exodus 34:28]. He did not eat or drink for forty days. You can die in the desert in 24 hours if without water. The forty days was enabled by God.
- ⇨ Elijah when he fled Jezebel he spent forty days without food. Before the forty days fast, an angel fed him with a special meal [1 Kings 19:5-8].
- ⇨ Jesus – After his baptism and the Holy Spirit anointing, he was led [driven] by the spirit into the wilderness to fast [Luke 4:1-2] and angels ministered to him afterwards. The Holy Spirit led him.

## Some Practical considerations
i. You may drink water when fasting. Matthew 4:1-2 [Luke 4:1-2] says, *"Afterwards he [Jesus] hungered"* not afterwards he thirsted.
ii. Dehydration due to extreme heat can cause permanent damage to your body, especially when one is not in good health. It is recommended to consult your medical practitioner, if you are to go for more than two days without fluids.

iii. Fasting can be dangerous. God's arm cannot be twisted by fasting. Forcing God to do something with questionable motive, or self-willed can open wrong spirits [since fasting brings you closer to the spiritual world].

iv. Fasting from food continually, longer than ten days can harm your health. Longer fast should only be under clear, certain direction, and miraculous enablement from the Lord. A number of people have so far died in a forty day fasts. There is no doubt that they were not lead by the Holy Spirit, but by human self-will. Longer fast needs the gift or the grace of God. When you have the gift you will not be hungry during the fast. Remember *"afterwards* [not during the fast] *he hungered."*

v. The motivation in fasting must be carefully weighed. Some press in for power and anointing prematurely and are destroyed by it since they seek out of self will. The anointing is a very dangerous thing. With unlimited power available to us, we would go out, and do lots of things, violating all kinds of divine principles, and doing lots of foolish things that would destroy us and the work of God.

### Spiritual Warfare
There are three sources of power:
1. Divine power – from the omnipotence of God.
2. Satanic power – from Satan the once Lucifer the fallen archangel.
3. Human power – power of men, and it is neutral. It can be directed by either heaven or demonic power.

Now the Bible says, *"And from the days of John the Baptist until the present time, the kingdom of heaven has endured violent assault, and violent men seize it by force [as a precious prize--a share in the heavenly kingdom is sought with most ardent zeal and intense exertion]"* [Matt 11:12 Amp]. John the Baptist was the forerunner of the kingdom of God on earth. Many people [Jews] repented from sins. When Jesus came he demonstrated that the kingdom of God had come though the miracles which he did. Even demons confessed that he was the son of God and begged him not to destroy them. Satan knew that his time was up and the children of God are coming to take what is theirs. But most Christians do neither know that they are in a battle, nor do they know how to fight in spiritual warfare.

*"My people are destroyed for lack of knowledge: because thou hast rejected knowledge, I will also reject thee"* [Hosea 4:6]. Jesus came to reveal to us the truth and he is the one who can set us free. *"And ye shall know the truth, and the truth shall make you free"* [John 8:32]. He said, *"The thief cometh not, but*

*for to steal, and to kill, and to destroy: I am come that they might have life, and that they might have it more abundantly"* [John 10:10]. The mission of the devil is to kill and destroy your life. In 1 Peter 5:8 we read the following, *"Be sober, be vigilant; because your adversary the devil, as a roaring lion, walketh about, seeking whom he may devour."* Satan does nothing but seeks to destroy you. We are part of a great war. It is a war between right and wrong. It is a war between light and darkness. It is a war between life and death. It is a war between faith and unbelief.

In this war our enemy, the Satan, goes around like a lion and he will kill everyone he can. John 8:44 says, *"..... He was a murderer from the beginning, and abode not in the truth, because there is no truth in him. When he speaketh a lie, he speaketh of his own: for he is a liar, and the father of it."* With all the power he possesses and all his trickery, he will try to kill us. He kills us by taking us away from God who gives life. He even tried to make the Lord Jesus Christ sin [Matt 4:1-11]. He will try everything in his power to defeat you.

## The Kingdom of God

Easton's Bible dictionary defines the 'Kingdom of God' as follows. [Matt. 6:33; Mark 1:14, 15; Luke 4:43] = *"kingdom of Christ"* [Matt. 13:41; 20:21] = *"kingdom of Christ and of God"* [Eph. 5:5] = *"kingdom of David"* [Mark 11:10] = *"the kingdom"* [Matt. 8:12; 13:19] = *"kingdom of heaven"* [Matt. 3:2; 4:17; 13:41], all denote the same thing under different aspects, viz.: (1) Christ's mediatorial authority, or his rule on the earth; (2) the blessings and advantages of all kinds that flow from this rule; (3) the subjects of this kingdom taken collectively, or the Church.

Since the days of John the Baptist the kingdom of God has been forcefully advancing. Christ preached the gospel [Good News] of the kingdom of God. *"The time has come,"* Jesus preached *"the Kingdom of God is near. Repent and believe the Good News."* Jesus meant that, 'the authority of God has come to claim what is rightfully his.' This is why Christ's pattern of ministry was offensive: 1) Proclamation: He preached repentance and the Good News of the kingdom of God. 2) Demonstration: He cast out demons , healed the sick, raised the dead etc.

The kingdom of God consists of Christians. Jesus told Peter that *"the gates of hell shall not prevail against it* (the church)*"* [Matt 16:18]. The gates of hell are the stronghold of evil and death, satanic powers that seek to destroy

Christians. *"For we wrestle not against flesh and blood, but against principalities, against powers, against the rulers of the darkness of this world, against spiritual wickedness in high places."* [Eph 6:12]. Entering the kingdom of God (being born again) is like enlisting in the army. A worldwide army was born from the Pentecost power encounter. Jesus did not die for a cosmetic Christianity but, *"Then he called his twelve disciples together, and gave them power and authority over all devils, and to cure diseases."* [Luke 9:1].

There are no demilitarised zones. We are born (again) into the war and unless the day of the Lord comes, we die in the fight. The kingdom of Satan is Christ's real enemy. Our mission is to rescue that which has been taken captive by the devil. The final outcome of the battle was assured through Christ's death on the cross, resurrection and ascension. Until Christ comes we fight. We are God's army. Like it or not the devil will fight you. His goal is to burn our draft cards and make us AWOL. Satan is the destroyer, the deceiver, the father of lies and the butcher of the world. He has no rules of war. Nothing for him is fair and he is not a gentleman. Any attempt to make peace with him will be a win, lose deal in his favour.

But we are not unaware of his schemes. Satan attacks on three major fronts:

i.   **The Flesh.** Our sinful passions that reside within us are sources of temptation. *"For I know that in me (that is, in my flesh,) dwelleth no good thing"* [Rom 7:18]. *"This I say then, Walk in the Spirit, and ye shall not fulfil the lust of the flesh"* [Gal 5:16]. Resist the devil and he will flee from you.

ii.  **The World.** *"Now therefore ye are no more strangers and foreigners, but fellow citizens with the saints, and of the household of God"* [Eph 2:19]. A Christian is an ambassador of the kingdom of heaven on earth. How can a Christian serve God's kingdom while taking on the values and lifestyle of the world (that is, Satan's kingdom) he/she wants to transform? They cannot. *"No man that warreth then tangles himself with the affairs of this life; that he may please him who hath chosen him to be a soldier"* [2Tim 2:4]. Fellowship with other is a vital defence against being swept by the world. Prayer, studying the word of God and spiritual discipline like fasting are necessary to empower us (load our spiritual guns) and gain insight but also for equipping us to overcome the world.

iii. **The Devil.** He inflicts us with diseases and attacks us spiritually. *"The thief cometh not, but for to steal, and to kill, and to destroy: I am come that they might have life, and that they might have it more abundantly"* [John 10:10]. We war against the devil and his demons, not men.

Although we are in a war, we fight from victory because Jesus won the war on the cross. Our fight is a matter of enforcing the victory. We are just taking over areas of resistance using our authority from the fact that we won the war on the cross.

## Victory is yours

You can never walk in victory until you are sure your enemy is defeated. *"And having spoiled principalities and powers, he made a shew of them openly, triumphing over them in it"* [Col 2:15]. This means that the devil was defeated on the cross of Calvary. Jesus gave us authority over the devil. *"And the seventy returned again with joy, saying, Lord, even the devils are subject unto us through thy name. And he said unto them, I beheld Satan as lightning fall from heaven. Behold, I give unto you power to tread on serpents and scorpions, and over all the power of the enemy: and nothing shall by any means hurt you"* [Luke 10:17-19]. Do not retreat. *"Be sober, be vigilant; because your adversary the devil, as a roaring lion, walketh about, seeking whom he may devour"* [1Peter 5:8]. The devil pretends to be a lion whilst Jesus, 'the true lion of the tribe of Judah' is the real lion. *"The wicked flee when no man pursueth: but the righteous are bold as a lion"* [Prov 28:1]. Be bold and run towards the roar. The devil's roar is to frighten us, but he is toothless and disarmed. A roar cannot bite, but scare you.

The devil has power but does not have authority. Jesus gave us the authority and the power. This puts us in a position to have authority over the devil's power. We can shut him down if we want. Now authority works by faith. Satan sows seeds of doubt and fear into the ground of our hearts and minds. If we cultivate or nurture these seeds, they can grow in to very large weeds. Resist the devil. Stand firm in faith, by the authority of God's word and the power of God's Spirit. *"Heaven and earth shall pass away: but my words shall not pass away"* [Luke 21:33]. Speak the word in faith to God in prayer, in confession of our mouth and to the devil in reproof.

*"And they overcame him by the blood of the Lamb, and by the word of their testimony; and they loved not their lives unto the death"* [Rev 12:11]. At Calvary, Jesus Christ the lion of Judah defeated the devil and stripped him of his power. That's why, *"the devil also believe and (but) tremble."* Fear attracts evil power, but faith brings God into our daily lives. Fear is the opposite of faith.

Before he left Jesus said, *"..... These things I have spoken unto you, that in me ye might have peace. In the world ye shall have tribulation: but be of good cheer; I have overcome the world"* [John 16:33]. *Jesus is the Lord of victory. The power of the enemy has been broken forever. The devil has been defeated.* *"But the saints of the most High shall take the kingdom, and possess the kingdom forever, even forever and ever"* [Dan 7:18].

As you fight the good fight of faith and set the prisoner free, keep in touch with Jesus Christ the commander-in-chief. Keep listening for instructions day-by-day by living a God guided life. God desire to speak and is speaking to you right now. Be still and hear His voice. Allow Him to direct your path and to live in victory.

## 14. PRAISE AND WORSHIP

### What is Praise?

Praise is an expression of admiration and appreciation. When we praise someone we tell Him how wonderful [we think] he is, or how great his accomplishments are. It is the same with God. All true praise has something to do with acknowledging and focusing on God's nature, character and power. It has elements of complimenting, glorifying, honouring and exalting God. Praise also involves joyful thanking and adoring of God, and celebration of his goodness and grace.

To have effective praise we need to understand the attitude of God, the object of our praise. We have to know God. As we praise we focus on God's; self-sufficiency, eternity, totality, love, presence, greatness, glory, uniqueness, holiness, Excellency, strength, reliability, majesty, creativity, generosity, ability, justice, beauty, kindness, forgiveness, faithfulness, powerfulness, righteousness, mercifulness, joy, stability, wonderfulness, truthfulness, patience, completeness, grace, victory, goodness, etc. The list is endless. There are so many things to praise God for.

### Elements of Praise

These are Old Testament Hebrew words which translated means "praise":

❖ Barak – to kneel in adoration.
❖ Hallah – to provide a clear sound, to boast, to celebrate, to rave about, to glory in.
❖ Hilluw – celebration of thanks giving for the completion of harvest and include singing and dancing.
❖ Shabach – shout with a loud voice, a shout of triumph, of glorying in the victory.
❖ Tehillah – sing forth a clear song of praise to God.
❖ Towdah – the extension of hands in adoration and thanksgiving.
❖ Yadah – to give forth a confession of thanks.
❖ Zamar – to touch or play the strings. Singing praise to the accompaniment of musical instruments.

Praise has something to do with:

❖ Physical expression – physical enactment and demonstration of spiritual perceptions.

❖ Audible sound – it involves shouting to God except in Barak when you kneel in adoration.

❖ Physical action – praise demands active physical participation.

❖ Emotional release – "Bless the Lord, O my soul: and all that is within me, bless his holy name" [Ps 103:1]. Praising God is not an emotional exercise but still there is freedom to express one's emotions.

### Why should we praise God?
God commanded us to praise him. In Psalm 47:7 says, *"For God is the King of all the earth: sing ye praises with understanding."* Absence of praise is disobedience. We praise Him because of who he is. *"Great is the Lord, and greatly to be praised in the city of our God, in the mountain of his holiness"* [Psalms 48:1]. He is the Lord, the king of kings and the Lord of Lords. Praise glorifies God. *"Whoso offereth praise glorifieth me: and to Him that ordereth his conversation aright will I shew the salvation of God"* [Psalms 50:23]. We also praise Him for all his benefits and his goodness. *"Bless the Lord, O my soul, and forget not all his benefits"* [Psalms 103:2]. *"Oh that men would praise the Lord for his goodness, and for his wonderful works to the children of men!"* [Psalms 107:8]. Praise brings God's power [Psalms 84:4-7]. People who consistently praise God move from strength to strength. Praise exceeds victory. In 2 Chronicles 20:21-22, King Jehoshaphat and the people defeated the enemy through praise.

### Praise; a Weapon in spiritual Warfare
The power of praise is a weapon in spiritual warfare. *"For the weapons of our warfare are not carnal, but mighty through God to the pulling down of strongholds"* [2Cor 10:4]. All victories, whether the result is an instantaneous deliverance from a circumstance or simply strength to endure a long difficult trial, flow from God's nature and character alone. God's manifest presence is our victory, and praise makes room for the fullness of his presence. *"But thou art holy, O thou that inhabits the praises of Israel"* [Psalms 22:3]. If God inhabits our praise then, praising saturates the circumstance with God's manifest presence. God set up his throne or dwells where his people praise him. We say a herd of cattle, a congregation of Christians, but we say a 'palace of praise.' Because it is God's dwelling place. Satan cannot operate in God's manifest presence. In 2 Chronicles 5:13-14 during the dedication of the

temple, the Israelites praised the Lord such, that the manifest presence of God filled the temple.

We do not praise God only after a victory but we praise Him also for future victories. This shows that we have faith in God's ability to deliver and we believe he will intervene on our behalf. Hence praising in midst of difficulty demonstrates and indicate the measure of our faith in God. Satan's chief desire is that God's children will minimize the greatness of God, while mentally maximising Satan's greatness. But praise diminishes the devil.

*"And if ye go to war in your land against the enemy that oppressed you, then ye shall blow an alarm with the trumpets; and ye shall be remembered before the Lord your God and ye shall be saved from your enemies. Also in the day of your gladness, and in your solemn days, and in the beginnings of your months, ye shall blow with the trumpets over your burnt offerings, and over the sacrifices of your peace offerings; that they may be to you for a memorial before your God: I am the Lord your God. ....... In the first place went the standard of the camp of the children of Judah according to their armies: and over his host was Nahshon the son of Amminadab"* [Num 10:9-14].

When the Israelites were going for war, they would firstly sound blasts or trumpets as a war cry. In other words, it is a shout of praise to God. The Israelites would saturate their warfare with praise, so that God would manifest in their midst and fight for them. They would also let the tribe of Judah go first. The name Judah means 'praise the Lord' in Hebrew [Gen 29:35]. Because of his name he became the leader of the twelve sons of Israel. In Judge 1:1-3 and 20:18, Judah was to go first whenever they go for war. Praise was to go first. Today we have to praise God before he delivers us from our difficult or so called impossible situations. Let's praise God when things are difficult, when faced with sickness, when having financial crisis or having problems in our families. Let's shout praise offering to God when having problems at work places or having marriage problems. There is power in praise. Power to level your mountains. Power to extinguish every arrow of the devil. Power to set you free from any bondage. Power to gain victory over Satan.

Look how the power of praise manifested:
❑ The walls of Jericho fall because of praise. *"And it came to pass on the seventh day, that they rose early about the dawning of the day, and compassed the city after the same manner seven times: only on that day they compassed the city seven times. And it came to pass at the seventh*

*time, when the priests blew with the trumpets, Joshua said unto the people, Shout; for the Lord hath given you the city. And the city shall be accursed, even it, and all that are therein, to the Lord ...........So the people shouted when the priests blew with the trumpets: and it came to pass, when the people heard the sound of the trumpet, and the people shouted with a great shout, that the wall fell down flat, so that the people went up into the city, every man straight before him, and they took the city"* [Josh 6:15-20].

❑ King Jehoshaphat and the people defeated the enemy through praise. *"And when he had consulted with the people, he appointed singers unto the Lord, and that should praise the beauty of holiness, as they went out before the army, and to say, Praise the Lord; for his mercy endureth for ever. And when they began to sing and to praise, the Lord set ambushments against the children of Ammon, Moab, and mount Seir, which were come against Judah; and they were smitten"* [2 Chr 20:21-22].

❑ Paul and Silas walked out of the Philippian prison through praise. *"And at midnight Paul and Silas prayed, and sang praises unto God: and the prisoners heard them. And suddenly there was a great earthquake, so that the foundations of the prison were shaken: and immediately all the doors were opened, and every one's bands were loosed."* [Acts 16:25-26].

❑ David drove evil spirits from Saul using praise. *"And it came to pass, when the evil spirit from God was upon Saul, that David took a harp, and played with his hand: so Saul was refreshed, and was well, and the evil spirit departed from him"* [1 Sam 16:23].

## When Should we Praise God?

❖ At all times. *"I will bless the Lord at all times: his praise shall continually be in my mouth"* [Psalms 34:1].

❖ In times of depression. *"Why art thou cast down, O my soul? And why art thou disquieted within me? hope thou in God: for I shall yet praise him, who is the health of my countenance, and my God"* [Psalms 42:11]

❖ Among the people. *"I will praise thee, O Lord, among the people: I will sing unto thee among the nations"* [Psalms 57:9].

❖ All day long. *"From the rising of the sun unto the going down of the same the Lord's name is to be praised"* [Psalms 113:3]. *"Let my mouth be filled with thy praise and with thy honour all the day"* [Psalms 71:8].

❖ In everything. *"Giving thanks always for all things unto God and the Father in the name of our Lord Jesus Christ"* [Eph 5:20].

## What hinders us From Praising God?

There are many reasons why Christians do not praise God. The major reason is ignorance. *"My people are destroyed for lack of knowledge: because thou hast rejected knowledge, I will also reject thee, that thou shalt be no priest to me: seeing thou hast forgotten the law of thy God, I will also forget thy children"* [Hosea 4:6]. There are many people who do not know either the importance of praise or how to praise. They do not know which songs to sing and how to lead them. The Bible has vital information we need to know on praise.

One more major obstruction to praise is pride. There is no effective without humility. *"And when the chief priests and scribes saw the wonderful things that he did, and the children crying in the temple, and saying, Hosanna to the Son of David; they were sore displeased, And said unto him, Hearest thou what these say? And Jesus saith unto them, Yea; have ye never read, Out of the mouth of babes and sucklings thou hast perfected praise?"* [Matt 21:15-16]. Perfect praise comes from those with a heart like that of a child. In 1 Chronicles 15:29, King David danced for the Lord like a baby. This is the spirit we need, the spirit of praise. The greatest temptation of musicians is pride. And Lucifer the chief angel of worship fell due to pride.

## What is Worship?

Whilst praise in an expression of admiration and appreciation, worship is an expression of love and adoration. It is possible to admire someone and appreciate what they do without loving them. Worship has to do with our love for the Lord that is, giving Him our whole heart and life. We express our feelings towards God. This is why the greatest commandment is *"Thou shalt love the Lord thy God with all thy heart, and with all thy soul, and with all thy mind"* [Matt 22:37].

The Bible commands us to worship God. Israel was to worship God as Lord and Him alone. *"I am the Lord thy God, which have brought thee out of the land of Egypt, out of the house of bondage. Thou shalt have no other gods before me.Thou shalt not make unto thee any graven image, or any likeness of anything that is in heaven above, or that is in the earth beneath, or that is in the water under the earth: Thou shalt not bow down thyself to them, nor serve them: for I the Lord thy God am a jealous God, visiting the iniquity of the fathers upon the children unto the third and fourth generation of them that hate me; And showing mercy unto thousands of them that love me, and keep my commandments"* [Exodus 20:2-6]. *"Then saith Jesus unto him, Get thee hence, Satan: for it is written, Thou shalt worship the Lord thy God, and Him only shalt thou serve"* [Matt 4:10]. Psalms 95:6 says, *"O come, let us worship and bow down: let us kneel before the Lord our maker."* Everyone should worship God. Even if you do not want to, one day you will *"for all nations shall come and worship before thee; for thy judgments are made manifest"* [Rev 15:4].

### How Shall we Worship God?

We cannot pretend to worship God and hope to get away with it. *"But the hour cometh and now is, when the true worshippers shall worship the Father in spirit and in truth: for the Father seeketh such to worship him. God is a Spirit: and they that worship Him must worship Him in spirit and in truth"* [John 4:23-24]. When we worship we go into the spiritual mode. The Holy Spirit helps us to worship, for he is the Spirit of God. But now Jesus said I am the way, the truth and the life. Jesus is the truth. We need the Son, Jesus Christ, in order to worship God, the Father. It's through Jesus Christ that our sins are forgiven and *"worship the Lord in the beauty of holiness"* [Psalms 96:9]. These are some of the things which take place when we worship:

❖ **We stand to sing.** *"And the Levites, of the children of the Kohathites, and of the children of the Korhites, stood up to praise the Lord God of Israel with a loud voice on high"* [2 Chr 20:19]. We need to stand up and sing. *"After this I beheld, and, lo, a great multitude, which no man could number, of all nations, and kindreds, and people, and tongues, stood before the throne, and before the Lamb, clothed with white robes, and palms in their hands; And cried with a loud voice, saying, Salvation to our God which sitteth upon the throne, and unto the Lamb"* [Rev 7:9-10]. The greatest multitude stood before the throne and worship so do we.

❖ **We clap hands.** *"O clap your hands, all ye people; shout unto God with the voice of triumph"* [Psalms 47:1]. The Bible commands us to clap our hands in worship.

❖ **We lift our hands.** It is scriptural to lift our hands as we worship. Lifting hands generally is a sign of defeat. When we lift our hands to God, it is a sign of giving our lives and surrendering to Him in submission. It is not only a sign of trust in God, but of humility. Psalms 63:4 says, *"Thus will I bless Thee while I live: I will lift up my hands in Thy name."* We are to lift our hands. *"Lift up your hands in the sanctuary, and bless the Lord"* [Psalms 134:2]. *"I will therefore that men pray everywhere, lifting up holy hands, without wrath and doubting"* [1 Tim 2:8].

❖ **We dance before the Lord.** *"Praise ye the Lord. Sing unto the Lord a new song, and his praise in the congregation of saints. Let Israel rejoice in Him that made him: let the children of Zion be joyful in their King.Let them praise his name in the dance: let them sing praises unto Him with the timbrel and harp"* [Psalms 149:1-3]. King David danced for the Lord in praise. We will rejoice as we dance for him. Dancing is part of praise.

❖ **We pray and sing in tongues and our own languages.** *"For if I pray in an unknown tongue, my spirit prayed, but my understanding is unfruitful. What is it then? I will pray with the spirit, and I will pray with the understanding also: I will sing with the spirit, and I will sing with the understanding also"* [1Cor 14:14-15]. The Bible allows us to sing and pray in other tongues.

❖ **We prophecy and interpret unknown tongues.** *"Wherefore, brethren, covet to prophesy, and forbid not to speak with tongues"* [1Cor 14:39]. *"Follow after charity, and desire spiritual gifts, but rather that ye may prophesy. For he that speaketh in an unknown tongue speaketh not unto men, but unto God: for no man understandeth him; howbeit in the spirit he speaketh mysteries. But he that prophesies this speaketh unto men to edification, and exhortation, and comfort"* [1Cor 14:1-3]. *"If any man speak in an unknown tongue, let it be by two, or at the most by three, and that by course; and let one interpret"* [1Cor 14:27].

❖ **Musical instruments are part of worship service.** *"Praise Him with the sound of the trumpet: praise Him with the psaltery and harp. Praise Him with the tumbrel and dance: praise Him with stringed instruments and organs. Praise Him upon the loud cymbals: praise Him upon the high sounding cymbals"* [Psalms 150:3-5].

❖ **Each person in the congregation may pray at once.** *"And when they heard that, they lifted up their voice to God with one accord, and said, Lord, thou art God, which hast made heaven, and earth, and the sea, and all that in them is"* [Acts 4:24].

# 15.  FELLOWSHIP

## What is fellowship?

The Bible word 'fellowship' [*koinonia*in Greek] means sharing or having in common. Naturally, we share more with those who share with us and less with those who do not. That is, sharing is a friendly agreement. Christian fellowship is associated with other Christians, to worship God, share our lives and work out solutions to problems as an alliance.

*"Now the company of believers was of one heart and soul, and not one of them claimed that anything which he possessed was [exclusively] his own, but everything they had was in common {and} for the use of all"* [Acts 4:32 Amp]. Fellowship involves sharing things such that at the end we have one heart (spirit), one mind (way of thinking) and all things in common. Having the same heart and mind means having a communal feeling and essence, general nature, and a collective attitude. It also includes laying down lives like Priscilla and Aquila who risked their lives for Apostle Paul [Romans 16:3-4] as well as sharing in suffering. *"Notwithstanding ye have done well, that ye did communicate with my affliction"* [Phil 4:14]. Brotherhood is all about serving, building up and encouraging each other. We need each other. *"Iron sharpeneth iron; so a man sharpeneth the countenance of his friend"* [Prov 27:17].

## The Power of association

The principle of the 'power of association' states that you either hold yourself back or improve yourself based on the people you spent time with the most. This is because their values, ideas, beliefs and directions are always influencing you. Therefore if a child has Christian parents, brothers, sisters and family members, they often impart these values into his/her life, which is a blessing.

As we become adults, 'peers' become just as important as 'family' in the area of association. That's why there is 'peer pressure.' It can be positive or negative, making you grow forward or backwards in your Christian life. Who do you spent most time with and listen to most? Be honest with yourself. Are these people going in the direction you want to go? Do they have ideas, beliefs, experiences and encouragement to share that can help you move in the direction you want to go? If your answer is not yes, then you need to make some changes in your circle of friends. You need to get involved in Christian activities where you can get to meet new and different people who you can share common beliefs and goals. Disassociate with, and break away from people who influence you negatively. Also limit your association with some of them. Expand and improve association with good people. Purposefully selecting those with whom you will surround yourself with. Also choose your mentors, coaches and advisors.

Christianity is not about being a 'Lone Ranger' but about being a family. Everyone needs a support group. There is power in unity. There is power in numbers. Have people who can lift you up or support you when you stumble. It is a true saying that 'it is difficult to soar like an eagle if you hang out with the buzzards and chickens all the time.' Your character is moulded by the influence of your friends.

## Christian Fellowship
The church is a community so are its people. It is a kingdom community. In the light of community, Paul makes the point in Ephesians 2 that we are *"hath quickened us together"* [2:5], *"raised us up together"* [2:6], *"made us sit together"* [2:6] and *"building fitly framed together"* [2:21]. When one is in Christ he joins the family of God. There is no more individualism and isolation. The early church kept on steadfastly in the apostle's teaching, fellowship, the breaking of bread and prayer. This church grew fast because of fellowship. They were all of one mind, sympathetic, loving their as brethren, compassionate and humble hearted.

Can a Christian really fellowship with an unbeliever or a person of other religion? The Bible says, *"Can two walk together, except they be agreed?"*[Amos 3:3]. For a true communion, there has to be agreement of heart and mind. And to agree with a person of opposing belief is based on compromise, this then jeopardises the faith of the believer. *"Be ye not unequally yoked together with unbelievers: for what fellowship hath righteousness with unrighteousness? and what communion hath light with darkness?"* [2 Cor 6:14]. The Bible forbids a believer to be in a relation with a nonbeliever, because a believer identified with Christ, he/she cannot be identified with a nonbeliever. But *"For whosoever shall do the will of God, the same is my brother, and my sister, and mother."* [Mark 3:35]. Our interaction with non-Christians has one aim, to make them come to Christ. We must love them. God does not show prejudice, but in every nation he accepts those who fear him, and do what is right. In Christ there are no denominational boundaries and church name tags. In Christ we are one family, with one head Jesus Christ.

## How to Have Effective Fellowship

The foundation of Christian fellowship is the love that Christ gave us. Fellowship is based on commitment to one another. *"Be kindly affectionate one to another with brotherly love; in honour preferring one another"* [Rom 12:10]. This is the main prerequisite for true fellowship. Relationships are incredibly shallow and fragile in most local churches, lacking a sense of primary commitment to each other. Our commitment must be based on 'agape' [covenantal or sacrificial] love. Agape is one way love, which is love 'in spite of', not 'because of' and that one is willing to lay down his life. Your love someone no matter what he/she does to you. Even if the person becomes your enemy you still love him/her [John 15:12-13]. This is unconditional love. There is a genuine interest in others' wellbeing, with no hidden agenda, no masks or selfish motives. True fellowship is Christ centred [1 John 1:3-7]. It implies walking in the light. Open, honest and truthful with one another. Forgiveness is also important to build up strong fellowship. Asking for forgiveness from those we hurt is humbling, liberating, but painless. The Bible encourages us to confess our sins to others.

God is love. Love is the nature of God. Love can conquer anything. Love spreads, that is, it is contagious. Love gives warmth to our hearts. It is love that brings effective fellowship. Love builds relationships with people, rather than bridges. We need to love our fellow brethren. Love makes us pray for them. Love makes us listen compassionately to their problems. Love makes us give to our church members who do not have. Love makes us reach out to a sinning brother. *"And the second is like, namely this, Thou shalt love thy neighbour as thyself. There is none other commandment greater than these"* [Mark 12:31]. Love binds us together. And there is power in unity. We make fire using a number of logs. One piece of wood cannot make fire. We need each other.

What then can separate us from each other? Paul rationalises this in Ephesians 4:4-6. We are members of one body, that is, Jesus Christ. We have one spirit, the Holy Spirit dwelling in each one of us. We have one hope and motive, which is eternal life. We have one Lord, one faith [in Jesus], one baptism, one God and Father. We are all one. Unity is an important ingredient for experiencing the power of the Holy Spirit.

Here are some of the Biblical results of fellowship:
- ❖ Fear of God – Acts 2:43.
- ❖ Joy – Acts 2:46.
- ❖ Favour with all people – Acts 2:47.
- ❖ Additional new believers – Acts 2:47.
- ❖ Good leaders – 1 Cor 16:15-16.
- ❖ All needs supplied – Phil 4:19.

## Discipline in Church

The scripture clearly explains that those who are members or believers are to submit themselves to the authority of those who God has placed in leadership over the church body. Accordingly, any member of the church who is found to walk in a way unworthy of Christian conduct, contrary to the word of God, will be subjected to disciplining. The goal of all discipline is not to punish the offender for their sins, because it is God who Judges and punishes. The purpose is not to take revenge and chase away the offender from church. Disciplining is love in action. It restores a believer to God.

Matthew 18:15-17 gives the three stages of Christian discipline. The Bible says, in Luke 17:3, if our brother sins, we should rebuke him. If he repents we forgive him, and our discipline is successful. James 5:19-20 also says that if anyone among us goes astray from the truth, remember that whoever turns a sinner from the error of his way, saves his soul from death and cover a multitude of sins. After being rebuked, if the offender does not repent, we should take one or two other Christians (probably local church leaders) with us and talk to the sinner again. If the sinner repents, that settles the matter. However, if the sinner still continues to live in sin, we must not become discouraged. We should take the matter to the church. In most churches it means taking the issue to the church council. In others, it means talking to the congregation. In all of these cases they would pray for the sinner, and talk to him about the danger he is in. If this does not produces change of behaviour, we have to declare in front of the whole congregation that such a person is no longer a member of the church. Excommunication (cutting all communication with the church) is the last stage. The offender is free to attend church but not as a member. And it is done with the hope that one may repent and restored to fellowship [1 Tim 1:20].

As we discipline others let us remind ourselves that we often sin but through the grace of God we can be forgiven. Just like our Father in heaven lets us exercise discipline in grace.

## The Kingdom Community

Personal growth is only one aspect of our commitment to each other in the kingdom community. Personal transformation must result in social transformation. We are the salt and light in the society. There is pain on earth due to broken relationships. This may have resulted from economic, political, racial, social or marital instability. Our society has a culture of rejecting people. Healing is needed. Jesus Christ is the answer. He uses you to touch people in your community. These are the 'out cast,' the racially discriminated, the poor and the 'sinner.' All these are the people on Jesus' heart. How do you feel towards these church members? What are you doing to show the attitude of Christ to them? Jesus is counting on you to show his love to the suffering world. You are Jesus' body. You carry His love to the world.

# 16. GIVING AND CHARITY

## What is tithing?
Tithe is a tenth part of a person's income devoted to God. Therefore to tithe is to give a tenth of our income to the work of God. It is not to be the pastor's salary only, but given to the work of the Lord. But church leaders may live from the tithe funds [1 Cur 9:1-4]. The Law of Moses require that a tenth part of everything be given to the Levite and priests [Lev 27:30-32]. In Malachi 3 the Bible talks about giving tithe. God condemns Israel for not paying tithes. But still God promises to bless those who tithe. And those who do not tithe bring a curse upon themselves.

*"At the end of three years thou shalt bring forth all the tithe of thine increase the same year, and shalt lay it up within thy gates: And the Levite, (because he hath no part nor inheritance with thee,) and the stranger, and the fatherless, and the widow, which are within thy gates, shall come, and shall eat and be satisfied; that the Lord thy God may bless thee in all the work of thine hand which thou doest"* [Deut 14:28-29]. Money from tithes should also be used to support the poor, needy, orphans and widows. Levites used to present a tenth of the tithe received from the Israelites to the Lord [Num 18:25-32].

This was given to Aaron and then [after the death of Aaron] to the storerooms of the treasury [Neh10:38]. *"And all the tithe of the land, whether of the seed of the land, or of the fruit of the tree, is the Lord's: it is holy unto the Lord"* [Lev 27:30]. Tithe is holy before God, therefore should not be stolen from him. Not tithing is considered by God as an act of robbing [Malachi 3], since it is looting as God watches. It's rebellion, cheating and defrauding God of his consecrated possession.

## The Origin of Tithing
The Bible first mention tithing in Genesis 14:20 when Abraham was returning from defeating Kedorlaomer, and the kings allied with him. He gave Melchizedek, king of Jerusalem and priest of the most high God, a tenth of everything. The issue of tithing is mentioned again in Genesis 28:22 when Jacob promised to give his tithe to God. In the Law of Moses tithes were given to the Levites and priests, to put in the national treasury. Goods were sold and the cash stored. Treasurers and administrators were appointed to manage the

finances and assets. All cash received was recorded, and expenditures were planned.

The New Testament mentioned that teachers of the law and Pharisees used to tithe even tiny garden seeds [Matthew 23:23], but Jesus called them hypocrites because their hearts were not good before God. Since we received Christ we became the children of Abraham. We inherit the blessing of Abraham with the conditions attached to them. Actually God does not only own our tithe but everything were are, and we have. We live for him, all tithes belongs to God.

## How to Tithe

As we pay our tithes today, God promises his blessing [Mal 3]. It redeems the rest of our income and wealth. It shuts out the devourer from plundering our wealth.

Let's not just give out money but also give our hearts to God. What God really want is not just money but our hearts.

In Deuteronomy 26 God introduced tithe to the Israelites and He gave an outline of how to tithe. Deut 26:2-3 says, *"That thou shalt take of the first of all the fruit of the earth, which thou shalt bring of thy land that the Lord thy God giveth thee, and shalt put it in a basket, and shalt go unto the place which the Lord thy God shall choose to place his name there. And thou shalt go unto the priest that shall be in those days, and say unto him, I profess this day unto the Lord thy God, that I am come unto the country which the Lord sware unto our fathers for to give us."*

Today Jesus is our High Priest. So we present the 10 percent (first fruits) of our income before Him. we confess and pray for it as indicated in verse 5-10. Tithing is complete when we wait on the Lord over it as we pray. The blessing of God is received by faith, so as you tithe believe that you will receive the blessing. Do not delegate someone to pray for your tithe, do it yourself.

## Giving Freewill Offerings

Giving is something the Bible says we should be able to do cheerfully and enthusiastically. *"Every man according as he purposeth in his heart, so let him give; not grudgingly, or of necessity: for God loveth a cheerful giver"* [2 Cor 9:7]. When we give we do it with gladness, and not sadness and gloomy faces. Below are some Biblical principles of giving:

❖ **Giving reflects one's belief about God's ownership.** *"For the earth is the Lord's, and the fullness thereof"* [1 Cor 10:26]. We own nothing. Everyone was born naked with nothing. Everyone dies and goes with nothing. We are managers/stewards of what God owns. Paul quoted the Psalmist when he wrote the above verse. So the question is not, how much we give to God, but rather how much God's money should we keep for ourselves [Exodus 19:5, Job 41:11, Haggai 2:8].

❖ **Giving can be an act of worship to God.** *"But I have all, and abound: I am full, having received of Epaphroditus the things which were sent from you, an odour of a sweet smell, a sacrifice acceptable, well pleasing to God"* [Phil 4:18]. The gift Paul received for his ministry is compared to a sacrifice in worship of God. Giving expresses how we feel towards God.

❖ **Giving reflects faith in God's provision.** The proportion of income given may be an indication of how much we trust God to provide for us. In Mark 12:41-44, Jesus commanded the poor widow who gave *"all she owned, all she had to live on."*

❖ **Giving is to be generous.** The Macedonian Christians were generous, and became models of sacrificial giving, even though Paul describes them as living in 'deep poverty' [2 Cur 8:1-5]. Yet their poverty overflowed in the wealth of their liberality. They gave not only according to their ability but beyond their ability.

❖ **Giving reflects spiritual trustworthiness.** Jesus said, *"If therefore ye have not been faithful in the unrighteous mammon, who will commit to your trust the true riches?"* [Luke 16:11]. The use of our money is one indicator of our relationship with Christ and our commitment to him. Our bank accounts tell much about us.

❖ **Giving is an expression of love for God.** Paul said that giving to God should be measured in the heart, and that's the standard in our love for God. *"I speak not by commandment, but by occasion of the forwardness of others, and to prove the sincerity of your love"* [2 Cor 8:8]. *"Every man according as he purposeth in his heart, so let him give; not grudgingly, or of necessity: for God loveth a cheerful giver"* [2 Cor 9:7]. Our giving reflects our love for God.

❖ **Giving help meet human needs.** Members of the early church sold possessions in order to have money for those among them who were in need. *"And all that believed were together, and had all things common; And sold their possessions and goods, and parted them to all men, as every man had need"* [Acts 2:44-45]. As a result none remained in need. In Acts 4:32-37, we see a Biblical warrant for spontaneous offerings to meet legitimate needs.

❖ **Giving should be planned and systematic.** Paul gave directions on giving to the church, *"Now concerning the collection for the saints, as I have given order to the churches of Galatia, even so do ye.Upon the first day of the week let every one of you lay by him in store, as God hath prospered him, that there be no gatherings when I come"* [1 Cor 16:1-2].

❖ **Generous giving will be blessed.** If you have a giving nature, others will give to you, including God. God blesses generous giving. *"Give, and it shall be given unto you; good measure, pressed down, and shaken together, and running over, shall men give into your bosom. For with the same measure that ye mete withal it shall be measured to you again"* [Luke 6:38]. Mark 10:29-30, the Bible promises us a hundred fold blessing if we give for his kingdom. *"And Jesus answered and said, Verily I say unto you, There is no man that hath left house, or brethren, or sisters, or father, or mother, or wife, or children, or lands, for my sake, and the gospel's, But he shall receive an hundredfold now in this time, houses, and brethren, and sisters, and mothers, and children, and lands, with persecutions; and in the world to come eternal life"* [Mark 10:29-30]. When God's principles are believed and followed, cheerful and enthusiastic giving will be the result.

## Charity and Generosity

*"And all that believed were together, and had all things common; And sold their possessions and goods, and parted them to all men, as every man had need"* [Acts 2:44-45]. This scripture is an example from the early church. Christians should support the needy, whether destitute, widows, homeless, orphans, or those affected by natural disasters and also travelling ministries and sacrificial giving to others. Many people are lacking; maybe because of economic situations, loss of job, refugees [foreigners], debt or sickness. All these people need our love and support. The only thing they know about Jesus is through us. Giving is a proof of our love. *"But by an equality, that now at this time your abundance may be a supply for their want, that their abundance also may be a supply for your want: that there may be equality"* [2 Cor 8:14]. *"Wherefore show ye to them, and before the churches, the proof of your love, and of our boasting on your behalf"* [2Cor 8:24]. The Corinthian were supposed to give to Titus and his companion as a sign of loving them. We can give as a church, but we should also give as individuals as well. You can make a difference in your society. Reach out in practical ways to friends, families and communities devastated by violent conflicts, natural disasters, HIV or poverty. Help them cope through relationship breakdowns, life's threatening illnesses, losing someone they love.

In the Bible we see many examples of generous and sacrificial giving:
- ✓ Israel when the tabernacle was built – Exodus 36:5.
- ✓ Early church gave to the needy – Acts 4:34-35.
- ✓ Macedonian church gave out of its poverty – 2 Cor 8:1-15.
- ✓ Widow of Zarephath gave the last food to Elijah – 1 King 17:12-15.
- ✓ Mary of Bethany anointed Jesus with expensive perfume – Mathew 26:7-13.

*"When the Son of man shall come in his glory, and all the holy angels with him, then shall he sit upon the throne of his glory: And before Him shall be gathered all nations: and he shall separate them one from another, as a shepherd divided his sheep from the goats: And he shall set the sheep on his right hand, but the goats on the left. Then shall the King say unto them on his right hand, Come, ye blessed of my Father, inherit the kingdom prepared for you from the foundation of the world: For I was an hungered, and ye gave me meat: I was thirsty, and ye gave me drink: I was a stranger, and ye took me in: Naked, and ye clothed me: I was sick, and ye visited me: I was in prison, and ye came unto me. Then shall the righteous answer him, saying, Lord, when saw we thee hungry, and fed thee? Or thirsty, and gave thee drink? When saw we thee a stranger, and took thee in? Or naked, and clothed thee? Or when saw we thee sick, or in prison, and came unto thee? And the King shall answer and say unto them, Verily I say unto you, Inasmuch as ye have done it unto one of the least of these my brethren, ye have done it unto me. Then shall he say also unto them on the left hand, Depart from me, ye cursed, into everlasting fire, prepared for the devil and his angels: For I was an hungered, and ye gave me no meat: I was thirsty, and ye gave me no drink: I was a stranger, and ye took me not in: naked, and ye clothed me not: sick, and in prison, and ye visited me not. Then shall they also answer him, saying, Lord, when saw we thee anhungred, or athirst, or a stranger, or naked, or sick, or in prison, and did not minister unto thee? Then shall he answer them, saying, Verily I say unto you, Inasmuch as ye did it not to one of the least of these, ye did it not to me. And these shall go away into everlasting punishment: but the righteous into life eternal"* Matt 25:31-46].

*"And let us not be weary in well doing: for in due season we shall reap, if we faint not. As we have therefore opportunity, let us do good unto all men, especially unto them who are of the household of faith"* [Gal 6:9].

*"We then that are strong ought to bear the infirmities of the weak and not to please ourselves"* [Rom 15:1].

*"And above all things have fervent charity among yourselves: for charity shall cover the multitude of sins"* [1 Pet 4:8].

## God's Special Promises

❖ *"Bring ye all the tithes into the storehouse, that there may be meat in mine house, and prove me now herewith, saith the Lord of hosts, if I will not open you the windows of heaven, and pour you out a blessing, that there shall not be room enough to receive it"* [Mal 3:10]. God blesses those who tithe. It takes faith to believe that the 90% that remains after tithing, will be blesses enough to achieve more than 100% income without tithing. Divine economics can prove this. We receive from God's promise by faith.

❖ *"And he said unto him, Well, thou good servant: because thou hast been faithful in a very little, have thou authority over ten cities"* [Luke 19:17]. *"He that is faithful in that which is least is faithful also in much: and he that is unjust in the least is unjust also in much. If therefore ye have not been faithful in the unrighteous mammon, who will commit to your trust the true riches? And if ye have not been faithful in that which is another man's, who shall give you that which is your own? No servant can serve two masters: for either he will hate the one, and love the other; or else he will hold to the one, and despise the other. Ye cannot serve God and mammon"* [Luke 16:10-13]. If we are faithful with the little we have, God will bless us with more. Mammon is a demonic principality who controls much of the world's wealth. We obey what we love. *"Know ye not, that to whom ye yield yourselves servants to obey, his servants ye are to whom ye obey; whether of sin unto death, or of obedience unto righteousness?"* [Rom 6:16].

❖ *"Give, and it shall be given unto you; good measure, pressed down, and shaken together, and running over, shall men give into your bosom. For with the same measure that ye mete withal it shall be measured to you again"* [Luke 6:38]. Giving is not loosing but it's an investment. The poor need to give because they need God's blessing to break the curse of poverty. Remember that *"He which soweth sparingly shall reap also sparingly; and he which soweth bountifully shall reap also bountifully"* [2 Cor 9:6].

## Finally
There are many reasons why people do not pay tithes or give. Some of the reasons are seemingly right. But what does God says?

At times we see financial mismanagement, but let us not focus on man but God. It is to God you are accountable, and it is God who blesses you. Play your part well and God will play his part to you and also to those responsible for the mismanagement. It can be disappointing to know that the money you are giving is being mishandled. It is a way Satan uses to steal the blessing from you, by discouraging you from giving. At the end it is you who ends up mismanaging your blessing.

Also as you pay tax to the government, consider it as giving. Pray for your tax and all the contribution you make to the government. If you pay taxes cheerfully, praying and believing God, He will honour His word and bless you for it. Who knows, sending your blessed tax can turn around things in the government.

God does not stop blessing you just because of corruption and mishandling of finances. God honours your heart and your faith. Whether you know it or not, evil things will always happen in one way or another because we are living in an imperfect world, and sin is all around us. We also sin from time to time. Don't you? But it is by the grace of God that we keep on doing good, and even loving our enemies!

# 17.  SOUL WINNING

Effective soul winning, evangelism or witnessing [of Jesus Christ] is simply making the initiative to share the gospel of Jesus Christ in the power of the Holy Spirit, and leaving the results to God. It means declaring, preaching, bringing, announcing or proclaiming the gospel [Good News]. It is simply telling others about Christ. The word evangelism and gospel come from the same Greek word. In this chapter we will look at spreading the gospel of Jesus Christ. What it is and what is our part? Who is to preach the gospel?

What is the gospel? The gospel is the Good News. It is the good news that God has caused to happen that which he promised earlier through the prophets; the time of salvation has arrived. Jesus Christ the Messiah [Saviour] has come to release the people from the bondage of Satan and give them new life [Luke 4:18-19]. The gospel has power to transform. Paul said. *"For I am not ashamed of the Gospel (good news) {of Christ,} for it is God's power working unto salvation [for deliverance from eternal death] to everyone who believes {with} a personal trust {and} a confident surrender {and} firm reliance, to the Jew first and also to the Greek"* [Rom 1:16]. There is saving power in the gospel.

## Why Do We Evangelise
□ **Jesus is our example.** *"For the Son of man is come to seek and to save that which was lost"* [Luke 19:10]. We are Christians because we follow Jesus Christ. He went where people are, and preached the gospel of the kingdom of God every day. Jesus was and is thirsty for souls. His desire is that all may be saved and come to the knowledge of the truth.
□ **The labourers are few.** In Matthew 9:37, Jesus tells us to ask God to send more preachers. The early church followed Jesus by preaching daily in the temple and even in houses [Acts 5:42]. As they went about doing their daily work they witnessed Christ. Therefore, their church grew tremendously. Today's church can only afford to preach one day per week, on Sunday whilst sinners sin every day. Nightclubs and dance houses open every day whilst church opens its doors only once a week.
□ **The great commission.** *"And he said unto them, Go ye into all the world, and preach the gospel to every creature"* [Mark 16:15]. This is a command. God is seeking people to use and to be sent. It is not only the pastors' responsibility but every believer. Every believer is commissioned [Matt 28:20] and God promised to be with us. Jesus said, *"Follow me and I will*

*make you fishers of men."* We follow Jesus in order to bring others to Christ.
- ❏ **The harvest is great [Matt 9:37].** The church is outnumbered by those who need to hear the gospel. The labourers are few in the harvest field, outside the church where sinners are. The best place to fish is not in a fish pond, but out in the sea. It is out of the church where we find thieves, prostitutes and people of other religions. All these people do not go to church. Non-Christians do not go to church. Let's preach the gospel everywhere we are, in the shopping malls, in the streets, in prisons, in our homes, and during our everyday businesses. Everyone you see in the street needs Jesus. He died for each one of them. You are Jesus' mouth now. He is counting on you. Do not say I can't or I do not have time. You can give out brochures, sent a message, talk to your friend or invite someone to church. There are two methods of evangelism; mass evangelism and personal evangelism.

## Mass Evangelism
In Acts 2:14-41, Peter preached (his first sermon after the Holy Spirit had been poured) to a gathering of many people from all over the world. This is mass evangelism. One person addresses a large audience. This method is used in churches and crusades. It also needs planning and resources in the form of finance, and often a sound system.

## Personal Evangelism
In this method one person addresses another person. Philip preached to the Ethiopian Eunuch by personal evangelism [Acts 8:26]. If we invite people to church meetings few sinners come. So instead of taking people to church, we take the church to the people using personal evangelism. With this method we can reach the unreached. It is well known that in some communities up to 90% of the people never attend church. In a real sense, there are more people outside than inside the church. Personal evangelism has proven to be the most effective way of reaching people. Personal evangelism can either be programmatic evangelism or power evangelism. During programmatic personal evangelism each individual is taught a common way of addressing person, in most cases with the help of pamphlets. The approaches are random. Any person you meet is a target. In power evangelism, the Holy Spirit reveals to you the target, allowing the Holy Spirit to guide you even during the conversation. This may result in a miraculous demonstration of God's power. Jesus used this method to preach to the Samaritan women at the well [John 4].

In general during evangelism two processes occur, the natural and the supernatural. The natural process consists of the words spoken, materials being used or any information that a person receives through his senses. Whilst the supernatural process involves the spiritual component of the message which touches the human spirit and convicts the person. This is the part that has the power to transform a person [Rom 1:16] and is lacking in many of today's sermons.

## How to Witness

The Bible says, *"The fruit of the righteous is a tree of life; and he that winneth souls is wise"* [Prov 11:30]. And Dan 12:3 says, *"And they that are wise shall shine as the brightness of the firmament; and they that turn many to righteousness as the stars forever and ever."* The one who evangelises is considered to be wise and will shine as stars for ever in heaven. God sent angels to do other things but not to witness. Surprisingly enough in most cases people do not know how to evangelise (witness). The first thing one should understand is that everyone is a witness. Church leaders should realise that it is better to teach a man to fish that to fish for him. And many people catch more fish than a single person. Therefore everyone is to go fishing for the lost souls. If each member of the church wins a single person to the Lord then the church will double in size.

Many people are not saved because no one made the attempt to introduce them to Christ. Before any evangelism campaign, prayer is very important. We wrestle not against flesh and blood but against spiritual evil forces [Eph 6:12]. The souls are won in the spirit first before they manifest in the physical. Pray every day for God to lead you to people who he wants you to talk to. Having some knowledge of the person you intend to approach has some advantages. Let your light shine and attract people to Christ. *"Ye are the light of the world. A city that is set on a hill cannot be hidden. Neither do men light a candle, and put it under a bushel, but on a candlestick; nor it gives light unto all that are in the house. Let your light so shine before men, that they may see your good works, and glorify your Father which is in heaven"* [Matt 5:14-16]. When people see your good deeds they will want to follow Christ as well. If they ask you the reason of your joy, your discipline and all about your life, tell them it's Jesus. Make contact with people you want to win. Remember you are the 'salt of the earth.' Go where people are and influence them for Christ.

Frequently you have to initiate with a blessing or demonstrate with a deed. If the person is hungry, give him some food. Give them something. But do not just give help without communicating the word. You have to say something. People do not just get born again. There has to be some talking. Do not argue for the sake of arguing, otherwise you will fail to win the person to Christ. And you will be won to the world. Above all that we do, let our motive be love. Have true compassion on people [Matt 9:35-37]. Some of us have to change the way we see people, for God to use us effectively in soul winning. How do you see people? How do you respond to people? Some styles of evangelism used in the early times are listed below:

➢ **Confrontational style** – Acts 2:14. Peter stood fearlessly and challenged the crowd with the gospel just after Pentecost. This method is used in mass evangelism.

➢ **Intellectual style** – Acts 17:16-34. *"Now while Paul waited for them at Athens, his spirit was stirred in him, when he saw the city wholly given to idolatry. Therefore disputed him in the synagogue with the Jews, and with the devout persons, and in the market daily with them that met with him. Then certain philosophers of the Epicureans, and of the Stoicks, encountered him. And some said, what will this babbler say? Other some, He seemeth to be a setter forth of strange gods: because he preached unto them Jesus, and the resurrection. And they took him, and brought him unto Areopagus, saying, May we know what this new doctrine, whereof thou speaks, is? For thou bringest certain strange things to our ears: we would know therefore what these things mean. (For all the Athenians and strangers which were there spent their time in nothing else, but either to tell, or to hear some new thing.)"* [Acts 17:16-21]. Paul reasoned with philosophers using this approach.

➢ **Testimonial Style** – John 4:39. *"And many of the Samaritans of that city believed on Him for the saying of the woman, which testified, He told me all that I ever did"* [John 4:39]. Your testimony can make someone believe in Christ.

➢ **Relational Style** – Matthew 5:13-16, Luke 19:1-9. We are the salt of the earth and the light of the world. Jesus had to go and have supper at Zacchaeus' house in order to win him. Our relationships can influence people for Christ. Building bridges to link with people, not walls to hide yourself.

➢ **Miraculous Style** – Acts 5:12-14. Miracles confirm the word of God [Mark 16:20]. They also prove that Jesus who was preaching is Lord and verify God's support of evangelism. People will then believe in Christ.

➤ **Service Style** – Acts 9:36. Providing services to people can be used as a way of reaching people. Note the services that people are searching for, and offer them with the gospel. Help with their groceries or cleaning their car.

➤ **Invitation Style** – John 4:39. Bring someone to a place where the gospel is being preached. They will hear and be saved.

The aim of evangelism is to 'win them all for Christ' regardless of race, origin, status or background. This is the mission of the church, so that the gospel of the kingdom can be preached to all nations. Do not be left out in this end time gospel campaign. Matthew 24:14 says the whole world will hear the gospel, then the end will come. This is a prophecy fulfilling mission. And this is God's desire. We have the responsibility. Obey God's calling. Preach the word daily and at every opportunity that you find. Make it a habit. Preach it in season and out of season. Preach during the day and at night. Preach it before Jesus comes again.

# 18. BACKSLIDING

What is backsliding? It is generally known as falling away from faith. Other words which are related to backsliding are declining, degeneration or deteriorating in faith. It is also deserting, abandoning or withdrawing from faith. It also means to weaken, fade or die out spiritually. Backsliding normally happens a little at a time and not overnight. It takes time and effort, starting in a very insignificant way. When we hear of Christians failing into serious sin, it is result of a steady backing. A brick wall does not collapse in a heap without good reason, such as decaying mortar or crumbling foundations which took a long time. So is with backsliding.

There are many reasons why people fall. But the most common causes are, the desire of the flesh, the love of the world, persecution, times of testing, lacking of fellowship, rebellion and yielding to temptation. God judges and punishes those who backslide. In order to avoid backsliding, one has to depend and trust on God. It is Him who can keep us from falling [Judge 24]. Proverbs 3:5-6 says, *"Trust in the Lord with all thine heart; and lean not unto thine own understanding. In all thy ways acknowledge him, and he shall direct thy paths."* Total commitment and associating with other Christians is an antidote to backsliding. Reading the word of God and keep growing in Christian character preserves us spiritually. Grow from faith to faith and from glory to glory. Press towards the goal, to be more like Christ. How do Christians successfully backslide?

## Symptoms of Backsliding

1. **Prayer is abandoned.** This is the first thing but it is not done at once, and making sure there is a little publicity as possible. Sudden termination of prayer frightens ones conscience, so it is not done a little at a time as though not in a hurry. There will be excuses for being absent from prayer meetings, and the Christian try to be as busy as possible. Even doing Christian work. This gives less and less time for prayer. Prayer is then substituted by other Christian works and activities.
2. **Bible reading is stopped.** Also this is done gradually. Bible reading is hurried and often substituted by 'good' books. These books are then quietly phased out with time. More time is now spent reading 'important news' in the newspaper.

3. **Christian's fellowship is avoided.** All avenues and opportunities of fellowship are closed as gradually as possible, so that no one asks about ones whereabouts. When the person meets with other Christians, words to encourage others are replaced with other news and interesting things.
4. **Worldly spirit is invited.** This person will then get as much of worldly spirit as his conscience allows. This can be love of money in pretext of prosperity and lust through friendship with unbelievers calling it 'loving all people.'
5. **'I will catch up.** 'When all this is happening, the one backsliding always promises to mend and catch up latter. But this 'catching up' will then last forever. The thought of catching up assures one that this is not disobedience [sinning], but simply delaying obedience. The attitude of 'as long as I am not hurting anybody' gives the person 'security.'

What does the word of God say about all this reasoning? *"Thine own wickedness shall correct thee, and thy backslidings shall reprove thee: know therefore and see that it is an evil thing and bitter, that thou hast forsaken the Lord thy God, and that my fear is not in thee, saith the Lord God of hosts"* [Jer 2:19]. If you find yourself loving any pleasure more than your prayers, any person better than Christ, be alarmed your backsliding has now began, to avoid backsliding you need to do a spiritual evaluation regularly.

## A Spiritual Assessment for You
*"As ye have therefore received Christ Jesus the Lord, so walk ye in him: Rooted and built up in him, and established in the faith, as ye have been taught, abounding therein with thanksgiving"* [Col 2:6-7]. Ask yourself these questions and be honest with the answers.

- Do I obey the leaders?
- Do I visit my leaders frequently?
- Do I speak the truth?
- Do I swear?
- Do I attend all church meetings?
- Do I have personal devotion, Bible study, unhurried prayer, and do listen to God?
- Am I sexually pure indeed, word and thought?

- Am I known as a Christian?
- Is Christ more loved, or at least more respected because of the way I live?
- How many people have I caused to leave the church?
- Do I conceal my discipleship, because I am ashamed or just a coward

- What am I like at home?
- Do those who know me best, believe in me most?
- Am I thoughtful of those serving me every day?
- How do I treat my sister or brother?
- How do I treat my spouse's relative or my housemaids?
- Do my children really depend on, and trust me?
- Do I still love my wife as from the beginning?
- Do I submit to my husband as the head of the family?
- Am I open with my earnings to my wife?
- Do I criticise the church in front of my children?
- Do I call the family for devotion?
- What makes me critical of others; jealously, revenge, inferiority or hatefulness?

- How much money do I give to church compared to what I keep?
- Compare what I give in church to my spending on cinema, sport, personal hobby etc.
- What about tithing?
- Do I pay my debts?
- Do I pay my tithes?

- How long is it since I first become a Christian?
- Have I grown steadily with time?
- Can I see my progress in the last few years? Few months?
- How many people have I lead to Christ over the last two years?
- After all these years can I spent an hour in prayer?
- When I think of 'getting on in life,' do I only think of worldly things like bigger income, a better job, more expensive car, promotion etc?
- Or more of grace and more of God?

- How much of my life is really given to others?
- Not just my family or friends, other people who needs you?
- Do I honestly love them, and without hidden motives?
- Not just for them to join my church or share my view?
- What am I doing to bring peace on earth, make more people know Christ, fight evil etc?

No matter what happened to you or how you feel about your past, God loves you and He is ready to accept you. Your family, church or community can reject you because of your past, but God loves you, regardless of what you can do or cannot do. He will accept you whether you ask for His forgiveness or not. His arms are open to welcome you. The best way to go is to go to ask for God's grace and mercy. He knows you more than anyone else. He made you for a purpose, long before your family, church or community knew you. He is the reason for your existence. He is the one to run to!

# AFTERWORD

*"All has been heard; the end of the matter is: Fear God [revere and worship Him, knowing that He is] and keep His commandments, for this is the whole of man [the full, original purpose of his creation, the object of God's providence, the root of character, the foundation of all happiness, the adjustment to all inharmonious circumstances and conditions under the sun] {and} the whole [duty] for every man. For God shall bring every work into judgment, with every secret thing, whether it is good or evil"* [Eccl 12:13-14].

The fear [reverence] of the Lord is the beginning of wisdom. Heaven is a reality. We have a building from God, an eternal house in heaven, not built by human hands. So we fix our eyes not on what is seen, but on what is unseen. What is seen is temporary but what is unseen is eternal. We live by faith, not by sight. Our citizenship is in heaven. For here we do not have an enduring city, but we are looking for the city that is to come. Then the righteous will shine like the sun in the kingdom of their father. Nothing impure will ever enter it, nor will anyone who does what is shameful or deceitful, but only those whose names are written in the lamb's book of life.

So do not store up yourself treasures on earth, where moth and rust destroy, and where thieves break in and steal. But store up for yourself treasures in heaven. Our present sufferings are not worth compared with the glory that will be revealed in us.

Knowing all this, I urge you to live a life worthy of the calling you have received. Weak faith in the teacher cannot stir stronger faith in the student. It is difficult to soar like an eagle if you hang out with the buzzards and chickens all the time. We labour not in vain. Jesus never fails. The world is looking to us. They need someone to deliver them. This is the calling we received. And this is the work to which we have been called to. *"Go yee therefore and make disciples of all nations."*

# ABOUT THE AUTHOR

Taka Sande is an author, teacher of the Word of God and a social and economic entrepreneur who facilitates social, spiritual and economic development. He is the creator and Managing Editor of www.itsmyfootprint.com blog. He has been a church leader for over 15 years and is a leader at Hatfield Christian church, www.hatfield.co.za in Pretoria, South Africa.

Taka has a passion for making a difference by influencing and adding value to people's lives. He believes in living a result orientated and purpose driven life. He enjoys facilitating processes that advance and improve lives of people, spiritually, socially and economically; finding purpose, maximising potential and reaching the limit of ones calling.

He is an infrastructure specialist by profession. His qualifications include Project Management Professional (PMP), a BSc Civil Engineering degree, an MBA degree and a Diploma in Church Leadership.

He is married to Beatrice and they have two children Tanya and Tinashe. They are also spearheading projects to help churches and communities in Zimbabwe through the Zim Mission Project (ZMP), www.zimmissionproject.com.

You are welcome to connect at It's My Footprint on:
- Email - admin@itsmyfootprint.com
- It's My Footprint Blog - http://www.itsmyfootprint.com/
- Facebook Group–https://www.facebook.com/groups/174721272602912/
- Facebook Page–https://www.facebook.com/ItsMyFootprint
- Twitter, https://twitter.com/ItsMyFootprint